PRICE AND POWER
OF FREEDOM

To Celia

[signature]

To a Patriotic American

LISA U. VARTANIAN

ISBN: 978-1500263270

Book Design by: **Sel P (sel.designroom@gmail.com)**

Printed in the United States of America

This book is dedicated to my mother, for her vision, for our future to be better then hers, for making the tough decision to immigrate her family to the land of the opportunity.

ACKNOWLEDGMENT

Dozens of patriotic and political books fill the shelves of bookstores. Privileged to reside in this country for more than three decades and see all the drastic changes take place has prompted me to write this book from an immigrant's point of view. A wise immigrant woman from communist Cuba told me, "One has to walk the walk, so they can talk the talk."

20 percent of all proceeds from the sale of the book will be donated to the military veterans. My goal is to help the severely wounded vets get track chairs, through Bill O'Reilly's organization, in honor of their voluntary sacrifices for our freedom. I thank each and every reader for helping me make my dream, a reality, one book at a time!

TABLE OF CONTENTS

In the first place, we should insist that if the immigrant who comes here in good faith becomes an American and assimilates himself to us, he shall be treated on an exact equality with everyone else, for it is an outrage to discriminate against any such man because of creed, or birthplace, or origin. But this is predicated upon the person's becoming in every facet an American, and nothing but an American… There can be no divided allegiance here. Any man who says he is an American, but something else also, isn't an American at all. We have room for but one flag, the American flag…

We have room for but one language here, and that is the English language… and we have room for but one sole loyalty and that is a loyalty to the American people.

THEODORE ROOSEVELT, 1907

PROLOGUE

It is about 9:00 o'clock in the evening of January 30th, 1981 and our plane lands in Los Angeles from New York's Kennedy International airport. I am fifteen years old, sitting next to my father near a windowisle in the plane, dozing off, yet so full of excitement that my insides are about to explode, because our plane is actually landing in Los Angeles!!! Finally this is a dream come true for my dad who has waited over thirty two years to get out of Armenia, which is a republic of previous communist Soviet Union. My happiness is strictly imaginary. I don't know any different than what I have been exposed to in my young life, however my father being born and raised in Athens, Greece and immigrated to Armenia at the age of sixteen, in 1947, with his widowed mother, siblings, and hundreds of relatives and neighbors, all of Armenian descent, who immigrated to Greece from Turkey after the Armenian Genocide in the early 1920's. Several countries like Greece, France, Lebanon and Syria, to name a few, welcomed the Armenian immigrants legally, who had to flee the Turkish Government. Looking back to that historic day in 1981, history was unfolding right in front of me and I was too young to understand the full concept of our journey. I know I am cramping up too much information, but as the story unfolds, I promise I will reveal this semisweet, yet inspiring, immigrant's story.

When things go wrong don't
go with them.

ELVIS PRESLEY, ROCK IDOL

CHAPTER 1

FAMILY HISTORY

My beloved paternal grandmother, Turvanda Terzian (a Turkish name) was the youngest of six children, born into an upper-middle class Armenian family of Murad and Mariam Terzian, (which in Turkish means Tailor) in 1906 in the city of Adana, Turkey with an older sister named Araxia and four brothers, Setrak, Tiran, Misak and Levon. It was customary in Turkey to have surnames of the trade the family was in. My great grandparents were professional tailors and that's how they had the Terzian surname. My grandmother did not know her actual birth date, because apparently in her era people did not record birth dates, at least in that part of the world, they generally went by the season, like the harvesting of wheat. My grandmother's parents were all of pure Armenian blood with Turkish citizenship, which was forced upon them not because they willingly moved to Turkey but because around the 13th century A.D. the Turks evaded western Armenia and forced the total population to become Turkish citizens. So not to be treated as second class citizens, lots of families mostly spoke the Turkish language and even gave their children Turkish names to blend in with the locals. Through many challenges and hard work most Armenians became successful businessmen in Turkey and continued to thrive for several centuries, until the late 1800's Ottoman Empire was threatened by the success of the Armenians in their country, so they decided to increase the taxes on the Armenian merchants heavily. That was the beginning of what is known today as the 1st genocide of the nineteenth century, which to this day has not been recognized by the Turkish government. After heavy taxation for many years, Armenians, fed up with the injustices, began organized protests towards the Turkish Government. In retaliation the Turkish Government began mandatory collection of all guns legally owned by Turkish-Armenian citizens. According to my grandmother, tensions were rising sky high and her father decided to leave everything behind and move the family from Adana to Izmir, which is another Turkish smaller city, where he thinks they will be safer at least for a while, so around 1912 the family moves. Grandma was about six years old. She vividly remembered her mother covering her face with mud nervously, because it was very common for the Turkish soldiers to steal young beautiful girls from helpless parents. The family lived in Izmir for few years as refugees and after losing two of their son's lives (Misak and Levon) the grief-stricken family makes a big decision to move to Greece, where many Armenians are welcomed by the Greek Government, well aware of the hostilities by the Turkish Government towards the Armenians. My grandmother is in her mid teens during this move. The family gets established within the first few years and settles in Athens, Greece. After graduating high school my grandma meets my beloved grandfather, Ruben Uluhojayan, oldest of three children, a brother named Hakop (Jack) and half sister named Yegisabet. He comes from an upper class Armenian Family of Hakop and Hripsime Uluhojayan (the translation of this last name means educator) and soon they start a family. A little bit of background on the family. Right before Hakop Jr. is born my great grandfather Hakop Sr. dies. Within a few years, my great grandmother Hripsime remarries and has her youngest and only daughter Yegisabet. Unfortunately within a short period of time Yegisapet's father fell very ill and passed away. I do not have any information on Yegisapets father, but I do know that great grandma Hripsime does not remarry again and raises all three children on her own and decides that all of them should carry the surname Uluhojayan.

My grandparents have four children, my aunt Varduhi (Rose) being the oldest and the only daughter. Their second child Karapet dies as an infant suffering from high fevers in the late twenties and doctors were unable to help. If in a short sentence I can describe my grandmother's character, I particularly remember this story. When her infant son Karapet was very ill, my grandfather came home during lunch hour to check on the baby. Grandma offered him a cup of Armenian coffee and as she is serving the cup, her eyes were constantly on the crib where the baby was. She witnessed the infant's final breath and waited patiently until grandpa finished his cup before she broke the horrible news to him. They are blessed with two more sons, my father and uncle, respectively Jirair (Jerard) and Murad after my great grandpa. They are able to give their children a good loving home and carefree lives until the late thirties. My grandfather and his brother are heavily involved in Armenian politics and become one of the leaders of an Armenian organization known as (HNCHAG), which is a strong organization to this day, all around the world in the Armenian communities, to keep Armenian heritage amongst other political issues. This organization gets tricked into propagandas from the communist Soviet Union, led by then President Stalin, who has a brilliant idea to immigrate all Armenians from all over the world to bring prosperity to this third world country called Armenia which is the left over part (eastern section of Armenia)untouched by the Turks and saved by the Russians for their own territorial interest, making Armenia one of the fifteen republics of the former Soviet Union. In 1940 the 2nd World War begins and by 1941 a lot of European countries are in big trouble from Nazi Germany. Greece's economy suffers tremendously. My dad used to tell me stories about waking up in the morning and seeing dead people on the streets from starvation. This lasted about a year and my grandfather falls heavily ill from stress of not being able to provide for his family. One particular incident that I remember from my dad's stories is him coming across a horse carriage full of bags of wheat. My dad is about 11 years old and very hungry. He looks around and no one is there. He is already imagining my grandmother baking warm bread with it. He walks to the carriage to grab a bag and next thing he knows, this massive chain lands on his back and he does not know how long he lies there, unconscious, but when he wakes up he can barely breathe from the pain. I believe World War II confirms my grandfather's wishes to immigrate to Armenia. However, his unexpected death does not allow him to make his wish come true. His brother Hakop tirelessly continues their agenda. Lobbyists work tirelessly for years as well, until like a chain reaction these poor people leave their homes, businesses, communities, one more time for the love of their country, truly believing to better their lives. Very few and brave immigrants leave for Armenia in early 1930's, and a much bigger group departs in 1946, including some close friends of my family. These selfless people write hundreds of letters to the ones who have stayed behind begging them not to make the same mistake, naming deceased people in their letters telling them that they reunited with the deceased to send a strong message to stop the further outpour of people to that evil regime. (All letters were scanned under communism so immigrants had to watch every word they wrote). You think people would listen. Well, unfortunately, most did not! However, few families, one of them being my grandfather's sister Yegisapet, married to Haroutun Sarkissian, decide to move their family to the United States instead (wise move!).

Let there be no doubt about our unity in the defense of our most precious heritage – that democracy which is envied by those who rightly crave it and feared by those who wrongly deny its force.

MARTIN LUTHER KING, JR.

CHAPTER 2

HARSH REALITY

October of 1947, when my dad is 17 years of age the entire family from both my grandmother and grandfather's side immigrate on a boat to the coast of the Black Sea with dreams and excitement, only to find themselves in a third world country (one indication of many people covered in lice from head to toe) . No one in their wildest dreams could imagine the nightmare they got themselves into the moment they put their foot down in a small town in Armenia called Lake Sevan. All these people are put in tents in late October under freezing weather conditions, until the government decides what to do with them. After a few days of agonizing wait, a bus full of them including most of my family are driven to the capital city of Armenia and are shown some land for all immigrants to begin their new lives by beginning to build their homes, which, under communist rules are all governmental properties, yet the government expects few thousand rubles, once these people settle. My grandmother is scared to death as a young widow with the responsibility of two teenage sons, her elderly mother and her mother-in-law. She requests that her piece of land be situated between her brother and brother-in-law (her husband's brother). Her wish is granted. Early 1948 a major construction begins in the area of Marash/ Nork in the capital city of Yerevan. The family puts their blood and sweat into building their home as thousands of other families do. The conditions are overwhelmingly difficult with no water or electricity available. All these people are under the glow of candle light at nights and they have to carry the water by buckets from one location, which is about quarter mile from where my family's lot is. (They felt blessed, because others had to walk much further).

Imagine that? It is one thing to be a local resident and not know any better, but all these immigrants, who voluntarily left their comfortable lives behind for this?

The land is very rocky so it takes my family about three years to complete the construction of this tiny house, and in the mean time they try to adjust to their new life. Everyone is forced to become a Soviet Union Citizen and when their passports are issued they completely mess up our last name, just simply could not spell it correctly, so we became Uludzhyan from Uluhojayan and my dad's uncle was given the name Ulukojoyan. Correction of any paperwork was out of the question under Soviet Regime. Another huge mistake was made with my father's birth year, instead of 1930 they put down 1923, which workes in my family's favor. My father is saved from serving the Russian Army, so he takes a job in a shoe factory to become a shoemaker to support his mother and younger brother. As far young as he can remember he has had a passion to play the Greek instrument "bouzouki", which is similar to a banjo, except it has a pear shape head. His parents buy him a smaller version of bouzouki that is called mandolin, when he is five or six years old and he teaches himself how to play. Luckily he brings this instrument with him to Armenia and entertains himself and many others.

My father used to tell me stories of just trying to purchase a daily bread was almost impossible. People waited in long lines all night and if there was enough bread they would get it, and the quality was so poor that they could squeeze water out of it. The money was nowhere enough to make a living so my grandmother sells all jewelry and valuables to make ends meet. In 1952 my uncle is enlisted into the Russian Army, which was mandatory for three years at the age of 18. He is shipped to Vladivastok, Russia.

It is three long years before my grandmother can breathe sigh of relief when her youngest son returns from the army. In the meantime, my parents met each other (I will write more about my mother). They have a lot in common since my mother's family has also immigrated from a small town of Xanthy in Greece. In a short time they decide to get married despite my grandmother's wishes not to, for reasons of poverty. In 1953 my parents have a secret religious (Christian) ceremony in their tiny home, because religion is forbidden by the Soviets. The very first winter of their marriage they have to temporarily move with my aunt, (my dad's sister's family) because they do not have money to buy heating oil. My aunt is married to Shahen who agrees for his wife's family to move in with them for several months. They survive the brutal winter and in the meantime my mom became pregnant with my oldest sister. It is very customary to name newborns after the father's side of the grandparents, so naturally my sister is named Hripsime.

My father is the sole provider for the whole family and they barely make ends meet. Growing up, my mom never shared much of her life with us but

I do remember her talking to her friends about craving ice cream during her whole pregnancy and not being able to afford it. Between my grandmother and mom they are very busy doing household chores and most everything is done from scratch without electricity, water and natural gas. If there were any televisions sold in Armenia, my family certainly could not afford it. So their typical lives from morning until night is spent carrying buckets of water to be able to cook and wash clothes. As years go by everyone gets used to this harsh ordinary life and according to living standards, most live below poverty levels. In the meantime my aunt introduces my uncle to his wife, who comes from a well-off family and they get married and he moves in with his wife's family.

In Soviet regime there were no rental apartments (as mentioned earlier in the book supposedly the government provides people with apartments but it takes years, sometimes a decade, to qualify for these apartments) so most families are forced to live together with ten or more in two bedroom tiny homes without indoor bathroom facilities.(talk about third world country). In January of 1959 my parents have my middle sister and she is named after my grandmother's mother whose name is Mariam, but my aunt insists that she be named Marine, claiming that Mariam is too ancient a name. My older sister is kind of a tomboy, yet the middle sister was very fragile as a child so my mom spent little more time with her, then my older sister. Few more years go by and on May 5th of 1965 I arrived in this world as Yegisapet Uluhojayan, (named after my great aunt). By the way, all of naming decisions are controlled by grandma, which I did not know until later in life. I absolutely and passionately hated my name. Everyone teased me about it and I can't blame them. When I turned six years old, all on my own I announced to everyone that I was changing my name to Liza. No one took me seriously. The teasing and the harassment continued. I stuck my firm ground and announced once again that I simply would not respond to that ugly name, because my name is Liza. Once again my grandma came to my rescue and was the first person to call me Liza. My aunt followed and even suggested to penalize a dime to anyone who would not call me by my new name.

In the late 60's a sporting goods factory opens up near our home and to be able to provide for the family my mom takes a job there as a packager. So I am raised by my grandmother and get extremely attached to her. She is this most loving, "strong like a rock" woman, yet as gentle as humanly possible. As far back as my memory serves me I was very close to her. I felt protected and loved and just simply safe being with her. When my aunt's husband Shahen suddenly passed away in 1971 our entire family was beyond devastation. Remember from earlier chapter he was the uncle that helped my family move in with them. He brought this BMW three seater motorcycle from Greece and used it as a transportation method. My grandmother moved in with her daughter for moral support through difficult times, and since schools did not start until the age of seven I moved into my aunt's place with grandma. They only lived few kilometers away but to get to their house required two different transportations which took a little over an hour to get there. Some weekends my dad would come and bring me home so I could spend time with my family. In 1966 my dad's cousin (his uncle's son), who lived next door to my family is getting married. My great aunt from the United States (state of New York) decided to attend the wedding with her husband. They bring the wedding gown from America for the bride and I believe every single girl from our extended family who got married used this gown. There weren't any wedding stores that I could remember that people could buy gowns and even if there were people simply could not afford it. My great aunt's visit to Armenia was devastation to her, watching all her nieces and nephews and their families live in such poverty. She made a statement at one of the family gatherings that not even the poorest American family lives under the conditions that her entire family does in Armenia. Many years later, I read an article, that Ronald Reagan had toured with Russia's president, Mikhail Garbochov in a helicopter and pointed out to him that most American families had homes and at least a car parked in the driveway. Owning an automobile in Armenia was a big deal. I knew then, that what my great aunt had told the family was true!

In Armenia there were apparently stores called "dollar stores", which meant you could only spend US dollar and obviously this was only for the American tourists. My great aunt took everyone shopping, and promised that they all would get at least one item. It is hard to believe that when we immigrated to United States I passed one of the jackets to a younger family member that was passed down to me from my oldest sister. We cherished those pieces because we just could not afford new ones (the quality of those items were superior with a proud tag identifying the source (made in the USA). At a very young age I realized that communism was a troubled party. I remember heated political conversations between my dad and his uncle (my grandfather's brother). He was a wonderful person yet I did not quite understand his political views. Remember he was one of the organizers that brought all these people from Greece to Soviet Armenia.

So I figured he either was a stubborn man or very naïve. If the conversation got heated he would simply shake his hand in the air and leave the room. As a young child I interpreted him as not being able to defend his views further. Every time these conversations took place I would not join the neighborhood kids for an outside play, I would quietly sit in a corner and listen, hoping that no one would notice me. Growing up in the 1970's kids weren't allowed to sit with the adults during "important" conversations, so sometimes I got lucky and sometimes I did not, but I hung on to every word that was said and made decisions right there and then as to who was wrong. The town I grew up in was called Nork/Marash, which was named by the immigrants after a town in Turkey, where it was mostly populated by Armenians. It was a hillside and we lived on 7th street, the house address was #6. We did not have separate schools for different age groups. The high school education was for 10 years from the age of seven to seventeen. Kindergartens were really popular but not mandatory for kids under the age of seven and many mothers who had to work to support their families enrolled their children. I believe they were more daycare centers than anything beneficial to the development of the children. My mom tried to enroll me since she had to work. I only barely lasted a day. I just cried nonstop the entire time I was there only wanting to go home to my grandma.

In the town there were three tiny grocery stores, two vegetable stands and one bakery. We were pretty lucky because our house was kind of in the center of town. Since I was the youngest in the family I was constantly asked by my parents to run to the grocery store to buy the daily necessities, such as dairy products or other items. I gladly did it, because most items were priced with odd amounts such as 14 cents for a bottle of yogurt or 11 cents for each egg, etc. A pack of matches cost 1cent. So, for example, I would go to the store to buy two bottles of yogurt and hand the cashier 30 cents. Normally that would be the end of the transaction. They never gave any change back, but little old me I would ask to purchase two bottles of yogurt and two packs of matches. I would always get dirty looks but I would get my two cents back! And every time I would come home and proudly announce my victory at the grocery store! One would question the two cents dilemma. You have to understand we are talking about an average educated person making sixty rubles a month! The blue collar workers got at least double that and sometimes little more. So you know how the saying goes "every penny counts", it was never as true as in soviet Armenia. One of the chores I had every day was to buy the daily bread from the bakery, which was almost across the street from my school. The bread was baked at a main bakery in the city and it was supposed to have been delivered to our local store around 2 o'clock in the afternoon, which made sense for me to buy it after school. Most of the time I would end up waiting in line on an average of about hour and a half, sometimes more. The woman who ran the bakery was the meanest woman I have ever met in my life. She was like some kind of a dictator with mean face. She would scream at everyone to stay in line and "everyone would get their bread". I always got shoved out of line because of my size. I was only about ten or eleven years of age.

There were three different kinds of bread that was sold at the bakery. The kind my family enjoyed was the finger bread, which sold for 33 cents each. I would not dare ask for my change back from this evil woman. I really was scared of her. The bread buying commotion did not last very long, as did the actual bread. If somehow I did not get the bread for the day my parents would have to take the bus to the city for the daily bread. Most of the time I got lucky. This ordeal was very stressful for me, especially when I got shoved around and got kicked out of line. I could not understand how adults could be that careless towards a child. These stories also went on at vegetable stands and at the grocers, especially during the one and only holiday that people celebrated. THE New Year's Eve! Since communist were atheists, no Christmas, Easter or any other family days were celebrated. People would start shopping for new year's celebration in the early fall. Nuts were big for new years. Baggies passed on to kids, except they were so unaffordable. That was the only time we got to eat nuts. I remember my dad standing in line outside all night among hundreds of other people to buy meat during freezing temperature outside. People would burn tires to keep warm. One particular incident I remember, my dad was first in line on one of this meat buying ordeals and before the store doors opened up there was so much pushing around that his chest got slammed to the metal doors of the grocery store and knocked the wind out of him. This was the wonderful communistic system we lived day in and day out in one of the most powerful countries in the world. Most families could not make ends meet with both husband and wife working full time for the entire month and I am only talking about basic necessities such as food, toiletries, etc., not including clothes or anything else for that matter.

The ultimate measure of a man is not where he stands in a moment of comfort, but where he stands at times of challenge and controversy.

CHAPTER 3

IRON DOORS AJAR

In the early sixties after the death of Stalin the hopeful immigrants cautiously watched the iron gates of communism ease a bit. The brave ones started to dream that by some slim chance they could get out of the system and come to the dream land of the United States of America! The law required that in order to move to another country, one must have an immediate relative inviting them with a permanent visa to move to that country. The required paperwork would be submitted to the specific governmental agency and within a year or year and a half of processing time, acceptance or denial letter would be issued without any explanation and applicants wouldn't dare question the outcome. There was no limitation of applying with a six-month waiting period in between. Most did just that to get yet another denial letter, and the vicious cycle continued for years. HOWEVER, if the right person was paid under the table, miraculously there would be an acceptance letter issued. One can wonder where anyone would have money (from what you have read so far) and I am talking about two to three thousand rubles per person! Most blue collar workers got paid between 100 to 300 rubles a month. The educated, such as teachers, engineers, doctors, accountants, etc. received 60 to 120 rubles. No, I did not mistype! You do the math of an average person's annual salary. Thanks for bearing with me on this. I am getting there. This is important information for the reader to get as clear a picture as possible of the system. I challenge the Michael Moore types to live in communist Cuba (identical creation of the old soviets) for a while, like an average Cuban lives. According to communism they value the blue collar workers much more then the educated professionals. The symbol of hammer and an ox was on a red flag representing the blue collar worker. Go figure! No wonder the system collapsed. Hooray to that!!!!

So these naive immigrants living and breathing the system for a couple of decades got toughened up a bit and began to work for themselves secretly. Most of them worked for the governmental companies and worked out of the house in the evenings behind locked doors. Well, most immigrants had trades, such as jewelers, shoemakers, tailors, mechanics, hairdressers, etc. They decided that they were going to take advantage of the system and actually their crime was going to be "working for themselves". So they did! My grandmother's sister's family had moved to Lebanon after the 1st world war, so my family could have used the opportunity to get out of the communistic Armenia. However, my dad or the rest of the family would not have the guts to even consider the move, because of the close ties with literally tens if not hundreds of family members being left behind.

Wisdom has two parts:
1)-Having a lot to say.
2)-Not saying it.

CHAPTER 4

GROWING UP

Some say personality is in one's genes. That must be true, because I was never sat down to be explained right from wrong. I generally acted on my sane instinct. Since I hung out with grandma quite a bit, one very important lesson I learned from her was to think twice before speaking. The women in our block would get together on a weekly basis for morning coffee and of course there would be some gossip. If I were to be at home and before they spoke they would look at grandma completely ignoring me and ask if I would repeat the conversation. My grandma would assure them that I was to be completely trusted. I took her confidence in me very seriously! That has stuck with me all my life.

School came to me very easily. I hardly did any homework at home, yet I was an average "B" student. I have to admit, our curriculum was pretty tough. We studied foreign language for five years, either English, French or German. The students did not have a say on choice of language. It was according to classroom we were in. My classroom was to study French. My mom, with much agony, transferred me to a different classroom where English was the choice. Yet both my sisters had studied French. I believe deep down my mother knew that our days were numbered in that country.

Music schools were real popular in the soviet union, the way sports are here for kids.

So of course when I was about nine years old my mother enrolled me at music school to take piano lessons. I have to be honest it was the best thing that my mom could have done for me. I know this now, but back then I hated the endless practicing, however I tremendously enjoyed the musical literature class I had to take and the chorus where I was a soloist.

Just to kill summer boredom I accidentally stumbled on a book that changed my teenage life. Books became my life! If there is such thing as bookaholic, I was one at the age of thirteen. Oh how much I loved it! Life was great. All characters became my imaginary friends.

The truth is like a lion.
You don't have to
defend it.
Let it loose.
It will defend itself.

ST. AUGUSTINE

CHAPTER 5

COMMUNISM IN PROGRESS (PART I)

By late seventies "coming to America" rush was at its peak! It had become a routine for my parents to say goodbye to their family and friends at the train station headed towards Moscow, where families were put through "the eye of a needle", meaning they had to pass Soviet customs. Oh, do I have a story there or what!

First things first! By 1978 my parents had decided we were moving to the City of Angels, home of the movie stars, Los Angeles! Through interesting and some weird channels we were able to apply at the Department of immigration in Armenia to permanently move to United States. Both my grandmothers were going to move to the States with the family. I had an Uncle John (Hovannes) who was married to my mom's oldest sister, who happened to be an eastern Armenian and most importantly he had connections at the "KGB". The price for this connection was $3,000.00 Russian rubles per person. The only way we could pay this was to sell our home of thirty plus years that was built by my grandma and my dad. The meeting was arranged and this man in his early forties came to our home and introduce himself as agent of KGB. I remember being disgusted by his offerings and at the same time scared, but if that was the ticket to freedom, my family had my big silent vote! Remember I was only fourteen years old and once again I was not allowed to speak my opinion. One important condition was that upon delivery of the acceptance letter we would sell our house and pay him the eighteen thousand rubles ($18,000.00). I still get flabbergasted thinking of the amount of money we paid (illegally), but then again the whole system flabbergasted me.

Months were just dragging on once we officially applied and one beautiful summer day my mom just ran to the house and gave me this big hug with a huge smile on her face.

I thought she had gone crazy (she was not the most affectionate person in the world, which was the norm for her) until I saw the letter in her hand from the immigration office. The appointment date on this letter was going to decide our future. As promised by KGB agent we were cleared to relocate. I had gone to heaven, except I was not dead!

Sweet, sour, bitter, pungent,
all must be tasted.

CHINESE PROVERB

CHAPTER 6

PREPARATION

This memorable time was June of 1980. Moscow was in massive preparations for the summer Olympics. The American Embassy was located in the heart of the red square in Moscow. In order to create this imaginary city, the communists canceled all flights in and out of the city until the last Olympian had left, which meant delays for our move. In the meantime my parents were busy selling everything we owned, which was not much. The biggest investment was our house, which we were offered twenty-eight thousand rubles. My father agreed to the deal right away. Criticism arose by neighbors and relatives about the price being too low. My mother was not happy about the deal as well. Houses similar to ours were selling for more. That's when I realized my father was not the most confident man. The sale of the house was finalized when my dad collected the whole amount in cash and we got one final visit from the KGB agent for the collection of his dues. I was so happy not see him again!

According to Soviet immigration laws, each individual could convert only one hundred rubles into US dollars, which would be $97.00 dollars per person. The value of one ruble was 97cents. On the other hand, in the black market people converted five rubles for $1.00 US dollar. It was in the best interest of my parents to raise as much capital as possible to benefit from the black market conversion. There were few specific items on the "generous" list of the old Soviets, such as one hundred grams of black Russian caviar per person, photo camera, if married, a wedding band, no other jewelry whatsoever and some household items. The rest would be at the discretion of the immigration officer.

Things were slow, but taking place. By early fall our house was getting empty and the space was being filled with luggage. It appeared we were always at farewell dinners with family and friends. It was kind of hectic and at the same time good times for all of us. My mom's mother who lived with my older aunt was not in best of health. She unexpectedly passed away in October. I was not too close with her. I took her death lightly. My mom was naturally devastated.

Never look down on
anybody unless you are
helping him up.

JESSE JACKSON

CHAPTER 7

TASTE OF FREEDOM

It is New Years Eve 1980 and there are lots of people in our home for our last evening we get to spend with friends and family. Early next morning we have a train to catch to Moscow, which will take three days to get to our destination. We have the company of many immigrant families, which makes the journey a little less scary. It is almost like having a support group. My father's sister and brother are part of our journey, which will end for them in Moscow. Part of them accompanying us is to spend quality time with my grandmother (their mother). She is in her mid seventies with severe osteoporos's. No one knows if this will be their last time together. The second reason is, we have to pass Soviet customs! Any belongings that is not allowed according to Soviet communist customs my aunt or uncle will involuntarily inherit. Our belongings are in six small pieces of luggage. Our appointment day has arrived to visit the United States Embassy.

The impact that meeting left me as a teenager will never be forgotten until my last living day. We were greeted by this beautiful tall, slender American blond, whom I had only seen in my wildest dreams, who was treating us with such gentle kindness and respect that I did not think existed, especially to my almost folded-in-two grandmother. I felt so special, intimidated, shy and jubilant by these wonderful people called "Americans".

The problem with socialism
is that you
eventually run out of other
people's money.

MARGARET THATCHER

CHAPTER 8

COMMUNISM IN PROGRESS (PART II)

On a freezing cold January Moscow morning, 1981, the whole family headed to the airport to continue our journey to America through Italy. It is going to be my very first airplane flight, yet I can't get my mind off the Soviet customs passage. I have heard many horror stories. Interrogation style strip searches. I am very much scared! Yet, I am not accustomed to sharing my fears and feelings with anyone.

After what seems to be endless hours, I was taken into a room with two very serious Russian women, without any parental supervision, and I am ordered to undress. (Last Soviet intimidation I guess, looking for those hidden treasures?).

My face is burning hot and my hands feel like frozen icicles. I am thinking (thank God I have an olive, Mediterranean complexion) they can't read my nervousness through my skin color at least. Tears are around the corner of my scared eyes, yet I won't allow them to roll down my face. In the midst of all this I am trying to keep my head busy and thinking of the Americans I met at the Embassy and comparing them to the Russians. Like a robot I am motionlessly following orders. My feelings are all mixed up with strong humiliation and that burning sensation simply won't go away. For the life of me I can't remember the ending of that horror search, which surprises me. As far as I know my memory is like a computer. Generally I remember everything about my life in detail, such as dates, time, weather conditions, etc. As I am writing this chapter the moment of that search resurfaces and I shift my thoughts sharply. It makes me mad!!

I consider myself a very strong individual; however, there are some moments in life that I rather not dwell on.

Suffering is the tuition one
pays for a character degree.

RICHARD M. RAYNER, MD. SPARKPEOPLE.COM MEMBER

CHAPTER 9

AMAZING ITALY

Flying is not bad for me at all. In fact it makes me happy that I can now claim the experience. For the moment I have no one to brag to, but I will in my future letters to family and friends. I especially cannot wait to brag about my short term American friends, that I will never see again. The thought makes me sad.

My brain is overwhelmed with short term thoughts. If attention deficit was diagnosable I would be a strong candidate during our journey. As we fly, a familiar conversation comes to mind that I have heard many times from adults. Their strong advice is to be motionless and most importantly verb less until one is physically out of the Soviet airplane and grounds. "They can turn the plane around", was the strong advice. Well, that fear is all out, at least for me. We are in Italy! Hurray to that! Imagine that, I am in Rome, one of the most romantic European cities in the world. Not bad for someone who has never left my own little town. My first meal is a disaster. I realize that I am an annoyingly finicky eater. Pasta is on my bad list of foods. I understand our stay in Italy is short couple of days. I still think it is too many days, when you are a hormonal and hungry teenager.

Our stay is sponsored by a nonprofit organization. I am forever grateful to them!

The plan is to get some sightseeing, while in Italy.

My father came down with a bad case of the flu. I believe this whole experience is getting to him, especially when the Russian inspectors would not allow him to bring his bouzouki to the states with us, claiming that it is an antique item. Just as they would not allow my grandma to bring one piece of fine porcelain espresso cup with matching saucer, that was given to her as a gift set of six by her husband forty plus years ago. Throughout years of moving and use, there were only two pieces left. One was given to my aunt as a memory from her father and one was used by grandma several times a day. Lot of times she would enjoy her espresso and cry at the same time, remembering good times with her beloved husband.

Going back to our sightseeing! We are able to hop on a bus by exchanging one ruble Soviet coins that portrayed communistic symbols and the head of Lenin with some Italian communist party loving students. They seemed really nice guys. I tried to communicate with them about communism and their obsession for it and suggested that they go live there for a while to get the real feel of the party. I am not sure if they understood me, but I got a kick out of the experience of speaking or at least trying to speak this romantic language, mainly through hand motion.

Bottom line, we certainly were happy to put the coins into good use. The water fountains and the statues were great, but the most fascinating thing for me was the supermarkets full of beautifully wrapped food items. I just could not get over it. The bummer was that we could not buy any of it. We simply did not have any money. The exchange of one hundred rubles we got in Moscow was ninety seven US Dollars, times five adults equaled to four hundred eighty five dollars for our whole family to be exact. We needed every dime of it in the US. Imagine that! An entire family of six was legally moving to another country in another continent with under $500.00 in their pockets. By the way, I was not given the permission for the money exchange due to being under age. More rules and regulations!

To my surprise when we got back my mother had sold all six cameras and other household items through this Armenian/Italian street vendor and raised few more hundred dollars. She was very proud of her accomplishments and the whole family was jubilant to have been able to liquidate our merchandise for cash.

Before I knew it, we were in the airport again, ready to board the plane headed to New York. Some of the family's destination would end there. We had to say our goodbyes to this one particular family, who had started their journey just about the same time as us. I was not thinking about that at the moment, because I was experiencing more nice Americans. I honestly was touched by the kindness of these strangers. Since I was the only one from my family who spoke very broken English I got into conversation with a couple of middle aged men about our journey, next thing I knew I was offered an earplug set and some wonderful snacks. Just like the ones I had seen just a day ago in Italian supermarkets and dreamed of eating them. Next thing I knew we were doing more goodbyes in this huge airport. It looked more like a city to me. Gosh it was overwhelming, yet we had no time to remain overwhelmed. Another aircraft awaited our arrival to complete the long journey to Los Angeles. I remember doing our best to hurry to the terminal where we were directed, with my grandmother not being able to barely walk. It was quite nerve wracking. There was anxiety and panic on everyone's face. If we only could communicate with anyone, maybe we could have gotten a wheel chair for grandma. On another thought, even if we spoke the language we would not be familiar with such simple and humane request. After for what felt an eternity we were seated in the plane and I could certainly see the calmness take over everyone's faces, at least throughout the flight.

There is no difference between living and learning… it is impossible and misleading and harmful to think of them as being separate.

JOHN HOLT, AUTHOR

CHAPTER 10

FREEDOM AT LAST

My eyes opened up to a gentle tap on my shoulder. It was my father telling me excitedly to look out the window. We were minutes away from touchdown to the City of Angeles. That idealized dream, bigger than life, was at its final chapter. It was the feeling of the struggling actor receiving the Oscar, the scientist's dream come true, flying to the moon, president elect's inauguration moment. My heart was feeling all of that and more. And touchdown! Passenger's claps ringing became church bells to my ears. I had learned so much in just a short few days, simple appreciation of life's moments, just what I had experienced at a landing of an airplane.

We found ourselves waiting for our distant relative's arrival at the airport, in the meantime watching hundreds of families unite with visible emotions. By now about half an hour has passed and my heart is beating a little faster just watching, at the same time being very scared of the unknown. Fear is clearly setting in on every one of my family member's faces.

The saying "world is a small place" was proven to me at one of the most vulnerable moments in my life when one of my dad's childhood friends came right upon us. After few minutes of warm greetings he was ready to transfer the entire luggage into the back of his station wagon and take us all to his home. While this was in progress our relatives appeared! Everyone took a big sigh of relief! They were looking for us in another area of this gigantic airport. Moments later we found ourselves in the car driven to the great unknown. The money that my parents hung on to so tight served its true purpose when the following morning we rented a one bedroom furnished place. The sleeping arrangements were interesting, but hey, remember the past? Anything was acceptable, at least to me!

Since I had so much love for this great country I was really optimistic and very naïve about the whole transition.

We were officially legalized when we visited Social Security office and received our permanent cards. The next visit to a governmental office was to apply for welfare. It was explained to my parents that they would qualify for the assistance until I was the age of twenty-one! At the age of fifteen I simply could not comprehend the theory of this government, handing out checks to folks who never had contributed to this country in any way. All that was necessary was to have a minor child or children. None of us could fill out the necessary documents, so my parents were introduced to this Armenian gentleman who would complete the necessary paperwork in exchange of the first month's payment, which was about $400.00. At our most vulnerable time this creep took advantage of us.

There are only two ways to live your life. One is as though nothing is a miracle. The other is as if everything is.

ALBERT EINSTEIN, PHYSICIST

CHAPTER 11

REALITIES OF IMMIGRATION

School attendance was delayed for me due to requirement of utility bills, as proof of residency. I kept checking the mailbox several times a day for those darn utility bills. In the meantime my entertainment and comfort in life was food, especially the discovery of toast bread. I thought it was the coolest food to be eaten. We did not have a toaster and used our oven as such. It wasn't quite the same but I still enjoyed this new pleasure, ignoring the fact that I might have been having way too many slices.

Finally after four weeks we received our first gas bill and I was enrolled at the famous Hollywood High School. Scared and intimidated, I was an emotional basket case. The fact that I could not communicate the language was devastating to me, yet somehow I survived the first few days. I was enrolled in English-ESL (English as second language) classes. Big sigh of relief came over me as I met a few Armenian kids. Comprehension of all other classes was quite challenging, due to the language factor. Life was quite tough from a fifteen year olds perspective, even though I really wanted to be an optimist. Had I known what lie ahead, the current situation would have been literally a piece of cake.

No act of kindness,
no matter how small,
is ever wasted.

AESOP, GREEK AUTHOR

CHAPTER 12

NOT SO SWEET 16TH BIRTHDAY

My 16th birthday was around the corner. Where I came from, turning 16 was just like any other birthday. My annual gift from my parents was to invite a few of my classmates over. This birthday was going to be different. I did not have many friends. Somehow I still was feeling happy.

All of a sudden it was clear that something was bothering or wrong with my father. For weeks he had walked many miles cruising Hollywood Boulevard, especially the heart and soul of Hollywood, around Mann's Chinese theater, almost like a visit to a museum to analyze every corner of a certain artwork, except in this case he was reading all the names of world famous stars on the sidewalks.

Apparently he was having dizzy spells and it had gotten pretty bad where he no longer could control his walks. Within very short days and a couple of doctor's visits he was diagnosed with a terminal brain tumor. Shock and disbelief are the only words that come to mind. What my family went through the next coming months I will try to put it into words.

My father was clearly depressed or had developed an attention deficit. He physically was there, but sociologically in a foreign land. All communications with us had come to a dead halt. Cigarettes had replaced everyone and everything, including sleepless nights. My mother tried to put a happy face on for all of us and somehow that made it worse for me. I was literally sick to my stomach, yet we were given the silent treatment towards this devastating situation by my parents. This is how things were normally handled.

Our family was at the mercy of very few kind family members and friends for communication with the doctors and transportation to the hospital.

I had never experienced such sadness in my short little life, yet more was to follow! I had forgotten all about my birthday.

The best place to find a helping hand is at the end of your own arm.

SWEDISH PROVERB

CHAPTER 13

UNREASONABLE DREAMS?

Just like anything else even sad news settles down eventually. I had become somewhat accustomed to my daily life. Lonely commutes to school by bus (if I was lucky enough to have been given the money for bus fair) and schoolwork kept me quite busy. The bright side of not having money to ride the bus was about two miles walk each way to and from school, which did me good. Weekends were long and boring! I thought I could kill time by writing letters and discovered that I actually was pretty good at it.

My father was on chemotherapy and seemed to have been doing better. The terminal illness part was tucked away somewhere deep inside my brain and I refused to let myself even look there. That is how I handled reality, by pretending it was not in existence. I convinced myself to the point where my letters reflected it as well.

One of those unlucky or lucky days without the funds for a bus fair, my attention was struck by what I thought was the most beautiful dress I had ever seen in my life in a store window front. Without hesitation I went inside and with my broken English I asked the sales lady if I could try it on. It took no time for her to figure out my size and next moment I was gently being assisted to the fitting room. Her service was mesmerizing, and when the dress was on me, I felt like Cinderella. It was the perfect fit! At that moment nothing mattered to me in the whole entire world but that soft silk dress. I thought, why not? I can go home and ask my mom for the money. Amazing, isn't it? My walks from school to home should have been a clear indication that we simply did not have the money.

The answer was going to be clearly a big NO, still I was looking for a miracle. I explained the whole trying on the dress experience to my mom and then had the guts to ask her if I could actually have it.

It was a strong educational moment in my young life. One thing was crystal clear to me, I had to grow up real fast and be a provider. Solution was a job!

A smile is a curve that can
set a lot of things straight.

V. BORGE

CHAPTER 14

KIND AMERICANS

Summer of 1981 was a resultless job hunt. I practically had walked into every retail store on Hollywood for several miles on both sides of the Boulevard. Downside to my situation was lack of language, age, and above all no experience. Disappointment was taking its toll on me big time.

The impressive swimming pool that lay in the center of our apartment building would have been a good way to keep hot summer days cool, except I did not know how to swim and I hated my body. Getting into a swimsuit was out of the question, and lucky for me we could not afford one anyways, and so that problem was solved.

By late August the days were on a countdown for beginning of a new school year.

Since my father was paralyzed on half side of his body through the tumor's pressure on his brain, the hospital had assigned him on physical therapy.

We had access to Turkish television through high antenna on our rooftop back in Armenia. One old American classic that we were privileged to watch was "Tarzan the Ape Man". The physical therapist showed up at our apartment twice a week to help my father with his movements.

He had quite the resemblance of the great actor Johnny Weissmuller from the Tarzan movie, so every time he came over I imagined that we had a famous actor over at the apartment. I was the assigned translator for him and once again his kind patience mesmerized me.

The therapy seemed to have improved my father's movement somewhat, yet, he needed our help desperately. It was especially tough on my mom, since my father was tall and big. She bravely put a smiley face on for all of us, most of the time.

The smallest good deed is better than the grandest intention.

BARBARA WALTERS

CHAPTER 15

FIRST THANKSGIVING

Physical therapy treatments completed early autumn. One November morning I was awakened by my mom, asking me to be a translator. Within moments I discovered the reason for my translator services. In our tiny living room stood the kind physical therapist holding a huge box. Pleased and confused with his visit, I tried very hard to understand what he patiently was trying to tell me. I was so intimidated and overwhelmed by his kindness that within moments I found my twisted palms completely wet.

For what seemed to be a long time, he had managed to explain to me all about the Thanksgiving Holiday (at least I thought I understood everything he said). After our sincere and profuse thanks we opened the box, which contained a huge turkey with some of the trimmings. Our Thanksgiving dinner was not the greatest, but the impact the whole experience left me was priceless. To him it was a simple goodwill towards a poor immigrant family. To me, that simple gesture was the symbol of a free land and its wonderful people.

The shepherd always tries
to persuade the sheep that
their interest and his own are
the same.

STENDHAL, **19**TH CENTURY FRENCH WRITER

CHAPTER 16

UNFAMILIAR CHRISTMAS

Christmas, regretfully, was an unfamiliar holiday. After all, Armenians were the first race to accept Christianity, yet I did not know a thing about it (what a shame). The circumstances of communist regiment sucked out its importance and forbade our religion. What is surprising is the acceptance of our people not to try their hardest to teach the younger generations about Christianity. Jewish people come to mind, with all the hardship they have endured over thousands of years, yet their religion is as strong as ever for the majority.

New Years day being the biggest holiday, did not come fast enough. We the people could not wait for New Years Eve, don't even know why?

This is how it went back then. We did not throw parties or anything like that. My mom and most average families began preparations weeks if not months before, due to most basic items, such as eggs, butter and nuts being obsolete (you get the picture?). Every single eve of December 31st our table would be full of all kinds of food. The bad part of that was that every home we visited had pretty much the same food. People visited relatives, friends and neighbors and this went on for a couple of weeks, so after a day or two, most everyone got sick of the same old food, yet most could not wait until next year for all of it to begin all over again. People's happiness was the food that was on the table. That was good old communism. Here in the United States our first New Years Eve was not going to be that exciting, the grocery stores carried just about everything we needed for baking and cooking and with the little income we had from this generous government we could pretty much have it all in one day. Amazing isn't it? Well, it was for me! Dennis Miller said it best on one segment of Bill O'Reilly's "Factor" about communism. And I quote "They don't know what happiness is!"

Plant seeds of expectation in your mind; cultivate thoughts that anticipate achievement. Believe in yourself as being capable of overcoming all obstacles and weaknesses.

NORMAN VINCENT PEALE

CHAPTER 17

FIRST ANNIVERSARY IN THE UNITED STATES

Reality of being paralyzed and helpless was hitting my father faster than a falling rock. His deepest thoughts and dreams had vanished with his soul; however, if I could guess, he was really sorry he had made this life threatening move to the United States, and I was soooo sorry the way he felt. It is amazing to me how crystal clear it was back then, the difference between the two giant countries and the endless opportunities in this great "One Nation under God".

By early spring my father's condition was worsening rapidly. His seizures were strong and clear evidence of bad things to come. Oh, we were so scared and helpless!

School was my savior. I literally dreaded the 3:00 p.m. school bell. That meant it was time to go home and face reality. My way of dealing with this horrendous pain was to hide from it, except there was nowhere to hide. Early spring also meant another birthday was around the corner for me. It was hard to believe a one year anniversary of our arrival into this country had rolled by.

Here and there I would experience brief moments of happiness about my upcoming birthday, then reality would wipe it out faster than a moment.

The last awful seizure my father experienced landed him in the hospital in a coma.

Once again our hopeless visits to the hospital were at the mercy of kind relatives and friends. Frustration and anger had consumed me so much that I was having mild anxiety attacks and was clueless of what those were all about. Was I going to share my anxiety issues with anyone? Absolutely not! I didn't even know what anxiety attack was until later in life. All I knew was that all of a sudden I could not breathe. The more I tried, the harder my breathing would get, until it would be so exhausting that I would begin to yawn uncontrollably, tears rolling down my face and eventually my breathing would normalize. There was never the right time, plus it was unfamiliar to go to my mom with any issue, yes, even health!

Should you find yourself at a loss, wondering what life is all about and what your purpose is, be thankful. There are those who didn't live long enough to get the opportunity to wonder.

UNKNOWN

CHAPTER 18

YET ANOTHER SOUR BIRTHDAY

It was my 17th birthday on Wednesday, May the 5th, 1982. By now my dad had been in a coma for a couple of weeks. I thought to myself, despite the situation, I was entitled to be happy. After all I was only seventeen and it was my birthday. Sure enough a good friend at school handed me a wrapped package and wished me a happy birthday! I was ecstatic for the attention and the gift. I thought to myself, my entitlement to a happy day had come true. I could not wait to go home and show my gift to my family. For once, I was anxious to go home.

The moment I walked through our front door, creepy energy literally took over my body, yet naively I went on to open the gift box that I had carried happily in my hand all day. My grandmother was curled up in one corner of our living room, dressed in black as always. Somehow I chose to ignore her hoping to find a happier person, so I slowly walked to our one and only tiny bedroom, where my mom was mumbling something through her teary face about my father passing away earlier in the day. (As I am writing this chapter I find myself in a great emotional stage, due to losing my oldest sister to cancer only four weeks ago).

I believe right at that moment my mind went into shock. I remember my grandmother asking me to eat something around midnight. I had been sitting in the very corner of the bed since I had walked in earlier that day. My thoughts of the day are as clear as a thick morning ocean fog.

The future belongs to those
who prepare for
it today.

UNKNOWN AUTHOR

CHAPTER 19

IS THERE LIGHT AT THE END OF THE TUNNEL?

Finding a job at this point in my life was critical. The same friend who had been so kind to me on my birthday had just landed a checker's position at this not so giant grocery chain store with minimum wage. It happened to be owned by an Armenian family. She promised to check into the company's hiring status for me. Sure enough, within a few days I was to join her in her adventurous bus ride (more than one) from the west side of Hollywood towards Downtown Los Angeles for a job interview with her boss.

I was beyond nervous and scared. When we got there I was greeted by a kind gentleman, who greeted me in Armenian, for which I took a big sigh of relief.

My English speaking skills were far from conversational.

He started asking me questions and within minutes I was more relaxed, feeling a genuine, somewhat young, fatherly figure sitting in front of me. My intuition did not let me down, even at the age of seventeen. As the questioning continued he very gently wanted to know the reason of me being all in black. When he found out about my father's passing, he again very carefully brought it to my attention that I was too young to be dressed all in black to mourn his death. To my astonishment he advised to only dwell on the good times I had with him. I was stunned by his suggestions. I only had seen people very sad in these situations and I WAS feeling extremely sad myself, yet this stranger made me see things from a different angle.

Something had changed inside me after the interview. I felt that I knew this kind man for a long time.

To my surprise I was hired on the spot and offered training immediately. Within very short moments my nervous body was standing next to my friend by the register, trying to grasp everything that was going on.

The best years of your life are the ones in which you decide your problems are your own. You do not blame them on your mother, the ecology, or the president. You realize that you control your own destiny.

ALBERT ELLIS

CHAPTER 20

SWITCHED PARENTAL ROLES

Time was going pretty darn fast between school and work and I could not have been happier about it. Timing was perfect, since summer vacation was around the corner. I was energized more than ever in my entire teenage life. This assessment was validated when I was handed my first paycheck. The value of my hard earned dollar, especially the liberation from asking for money from my mom (only for bus fair) knowing that this money came from the government was humiliating beyond words. Thank god I did not understand the origin of these funds.

One thing was crystal clear. I had to do everything in my little power to get us out of our financial situation. I didn't consult any of my family members for their help or support. An instant unwavering decision was made. With an important goal in mind, waking up gave me a whole new meaning. The last day of school was the beginning of full time work. I never knew the meaning of discipline, until those paychecks started rolling in. Only minimal amount was spent, pretty much for bus fair. Even that was saved many times, once I got closer with a bunch of co-workers, who generously gave me rides home most evenings.

By Christmas of 1982 my confidence level was pretty high, mainly through my job and my earnings. Unfortunately high enough where I was lacking in school and I didn't even care that much. My boss (the owner of the grocery store) had given me a couple of raises praising me for my excellent performance at work and had asked me to refer responsible girls like myself for an opening of a new location, which I gladly had done. The sadness of all this was that my mom and I had switched roles. She completely trusted me on schoolwork and social life and at seventeen my best judgment had prioritized work over school. I was not failing or anything, I simply had prioritized work over school.

Experience is not what
happens to a man.
It is what a man does with
what happens to him.

CHAPTER 21

SELF RELIANCE ROCKS

My father's one year death anniversary was approaching fast. My aunt, uncle and his wife wanted to be with us around that time, specifically for my grandma (and this was an opportunity for them to come to the United States). This was huge news! It was a whole process for them through the Soviet system to get the approval to leave the country, but I am sure they would find a way (money ruled!) and that was not an issue, especially for my uncle.

It was clear to me that we were going to play host in the very near future for three adults for several weeks in a one bedroom apartment. The big question was, HOW? For starters our worn furnished distressed apartment was not exactly the Tajmahal you know! Without a doubt the old stuff had to go! By now I was the proud owner of a nice size stack of green dollars (about $3,000.00 worth). That was supposed to go towards an automobile purchase, however, there was going to be a change of plans.

Between school and work there was no time for me to go furniture shopping, but if I asked my sisters, they were glad to be of service. Once the modest furniture was decorated in our little apartment, it felt like home! Everyone was real happy and I was very proud of my accomplishment and ready for many more to make it happen! I wasn't praised or anything like that and it was strictly due to my mom's upbringing of us. (I asked her once in my adult life why she never showed much loving emotion towards any of us, and her translation of loving emotion would be spoiling a child). In another word, she was unapproachable. One thing is certain to me, she did love us unconditionally. Sadly, she did not know how to show it.

They who give have all
things; they who withhold
have nothing.

HINDU PROVERB

CHAPTER 22

REUNION

Unwaveringly, our kind relatives were there once again to give us a ride to the airport. It was a very emotional union for my grandma and her living children. Without a question we were going to do everything in our power to make their stay pleasant. That is part of our culture.

Sleeping arrangements were made for my sisters and me at my cousin's nearby larger apartment living room floor.

Entertaining our guests was not going to be challenging, beginning with the basics, such as verity ice cream. Taking them to the supermarket was entertainment itself. Remember, they were from the previous communistic Soviet Union, one of the greatest empires in the world, yet the dictators of the evil empire could care less about the simple humanitarian basics for its people. (Beginning with toilet paper, just a reminder from earlier chapter, just can't get over the fact).

My future paychecks were not going to end up cashed and stashed for a little while. My belief of the endless possibilities in the free world was so strong that it was crucially important to prove it to our guests, who were not as optimistic as I.

The principal is competing against yourself. It's about self-improvement, about being better than you were the day before.

STEVE YOUNG

CHAPTER 23

FREEDOM WINS

On May 5th, 1983, which was supposed to have been my 18th birthday, my mom was busy preparing for a big luncheon to commemorate my dad's first death anniversary. We were all to go to church early in the morning and serve lunch at the church provided hall for all who were there for us.

I was informed that I had to play guard and stay home to make sure we were not burglarized. I don't want to confuse the reader, we absolutely had no valuables. I was to protect the merchandise our guests had accumulated into a small mountain in one corner of our already cramped up bedroom. It contained simple items as packs and packs of gum to hundreds of articles of clothing, some they would sell and some for their families. You may wonder where the finances came from. Well, we certainly could not provide it. They had exchanged Russian five rubles to U.S. one dollar through private trading and did have couple thousand dollars in their possession. To clarify the formula, this is how it went. People who wanted to send money to their relatives back home, my uncle would give them Russian rubles and we would be given the U.S. dollar here and this was done strictly on verbal trust.

A rare opportunity arose one late evening between my uncle and me about the differences of two countries with the entire family playing spectators. It was quite strange to be what started as a conversation with my uncle, especially a political one, but it is like someone had given me wings. I could not for the life of me understand how a reasonable logical person could not see the benefits of a free democratic country. I also did not understand my only self being on the defensive.

I was never put in this situation and being so young I was getting very emotional.

My last sentence to him was "Look, from the age of seventeen I proudly have supported my family, including the purchase of all this furniture that fills the room. Where in the world is that possible except in this country for an immigrant family, like ours!" There was a long pause and I fought with every ounce of energy for those oncoming tears not to surface!

Our lives are a sum total of
the choices we have made.

WAYNE DYER

CHAPTER 24

WHERE THERE IS A WILL THERE IS A WAY IN THE FREE WORLD

Driving was constantly in my mind but buried somewhere in the bottom of my simple to be accomplished list. Since I was the youngest and my mom was the authority figure, I had to wait my turn to take driving lessons. At ten dollars an hour with minimum of dozen classes to master the art of driving, it was quite pricey for all three of us to take it at the same time.

By now I had made friends with bunch of kids, all Armenians, who were fortunate enough to drive their families beat-up cars and were willing to give some of us rides. My urge for driving was so great, that I dared myself to ask one of my friends for his help in teaching me. My brain had played with the idea for weeks and finally got the courage to do so. Conveniently I had mastered the driver's permit in no time and had the valid copy carefully placed inside my backpack. All I needed was for someone to be kind enough and help me. To my surprise, my friend had agreed. I decided it was best not to tell my family, at least not for the moment. Danger never crossed my mind. So it was set, every morning sharp at 7:30 A.M I hopped into the driver's seat and off we went to school. No facial muscle movement appeared on my serious face while I drove the few minute distance. In the meantime my oldest sister was taking her driving lessons and had managed to successfully pass the test and thank God, now we had a driver in the family. While our guests were with us, we managed to purchase an old Mercury Cougar that would hopefully serve its basic purpose.

In one of my many letters to my cousin, who was eleven months older then I and because I thought we were close, I had promised to purchase a really nice dress and send it to her with her parents.

We parked our brand new (at least to us) but what I thought was an almost falling apart white and green Mercury Cougar in the heart of Hollywood by

Vine Street, where all the nice stores proudly displayed their pricey and fine clothing. A bunch of us came out of it ready to take on the stores. It really did not matter that this shopping trip was not for me. I took great pride being able to make a nice purchase for someone very dear. It actually felt better than if I were buying it for myself. Hollywood Boulevard was under our restless feet for a couple of hours and the shopping experience was priceless. For what I thought was a well spent $100.00, this fine tan color silk dress with light gold trimming fit perfectly on a lifeless window model. Proudly caring the fancy bag while walking towards our car, we found our parking spot totally empty. It had been towed!

I declared to my family that I was ready for my driving exam and explained my crash courses.

The date of the driving test was scheduled and at the end of it all, numbness controlled my entire body. Miraculously I heard the instructor mumbling something about me passing the driving exam. Momentarily, the sky had opened up and sucked me up into the heavens!

Whatever you can do, or dream you can, begin it. Boldness has genius, power and magic in it.

GOETHE

CHAPTER 25

COVERING UP EMOTIONS

There is a big difference between happiness that comes from accomplishments and material items verses when one experiences true happiness of unconditional love from a strong supportive family! As an immigrant teenager I buried all real emotional love and support that I craved so deeply at the bottom of my soul, and was petrified to throw even a quick glance in that area. I remained petrified with the reality of our hopeless financial situation and the unspoken sadness that wrapped itself tightly around each and every one of us deep to the core.

On the outside, now that I had my driver's license, my thoughts were constantly about purchasing my own automobile. I was quite mesmerized by the car in the reruns of "Dukes of Hazards" I watched on our little 20 inch television set we had received as a gift from my grandma's cousin and his wife, who had immigrated to the states from Romania in the sixties. Understanding the meaning of the show was quite challenging, but watching that car every time made my heart beat a little faster. Patience and hard work was all I knew that would bring me close to hopefully purchasing a similar used car. It was going to be quite challenging due to limited financial resources. A good chunk of my paycheck usually went to buying groceries from the market where I worked. I did not mind it at all; on the contrary, I took pride in being able to provide for my family. The pit was when I had to carry several grocery bags on the bus.

Hard work spotlights the character of people: some turn up their sleeves, some turn up their noses, and some don't turn up at all.

SAM EWING, HUMORIST

CHAPTER 26

END TO WELFARE; YES!

In the meantime our family was offered a quite interesting proposal from my father's widowed uncle, who by now was well into his eighties and lived by himself in the Studio City area of San Fernando Valley. We were being offered, all five of us, to move with him at his three bedroom tiny house (compared to our apartment was actually quite large) in exchange for taking care of him. Given our financial situation, I thought the timing could not have been better and jumped into raising my strong opinion about it. Surprisingly my opinion had mattered. The negative impact on my mom and grandma never crossed my mind. Grief stricken by my father's untimely death, they were just barely settling in Hollywood with a few Armenian neighbors and walking distance relatives.

"Everything happens for a reason" saying implied in our situation quite well. The first thing I was going to attend to was to take our family off the welfare program, which was a constant bother for me.

Since all five of us in the family were females we definitely needed a strong male individual to help us, especially with the rental truck. I knew just the right person I could ask and count on.

This tough guy (of course Armenian) I had met short while back, was constantly asking me out. The attention and the idea that someone was interested in little old fat me was beyond flattering, though I knew I was too young to be dating. It stood against our traditional culture as well. I wanted more than anything to follow good old tradition, and I knew what happened to those girls who had boyfriends. The minute the parents found out, they were married off. Yes, as young as sixteen for the gals and about twenty for the guys. The average age was about eighteen or nineteen, but some girls did get married as young as sixteen, in twentieth century in the United States. While the American feminists were fighting hard for their wild freedoms, we were being rushed into marriages we were simply not ready for! (This is not a criticism but simply a fact).

We were deprived from growing up properly into adulthood. Most newlyweds lived with the guy's parents and sometime grandparents and siblings as well. This is how it was done for decades and beyond and since it was the norm for everyone, it did not seem to have been such a bad thing. The bottom line of all of this was that I was going to do everything in my power not to fall into that trap.

Going back to our move, this guy had a tough guy's image and was definitely the one for the task! When I asked him sheepishly, he was thrilled to be of service and a big sigh of relief engulfed my tense body. About late 1983 the U-HAUL truck was loaded up and we were leaving our tiny apartment behind, hopefully with all the sad memories of my father's illness and passing with it.

Energy creates energy.
It is by spending oneself that
one becomes rich.

SARAH BERNHARDT, ACTRESS

CHAPTER 27

SOMEBODY SLOW ME DOWN!

One of the greatest moments of my life was when I voluntarily walked into the governmental welfare office and kindly informed the unmoved clerk that there would be one less family depending on this great nation's generosity.(I expected some sort of congratulatory comment). In my wildest dream I could not imagine the many millions that would be so dependent on the system later on in life. To justify the situation, I constantly had to remind myself that if any family was qualified for the assistance it was us! Recently I watched the great film "Cinderella Man" (for anybody who has seen the movie) on a cable movie channel and experienced a very familiar and emotional flashback.

The move had gone quite smooth. Our great uncle was ecstatic for having family around all the time. Living in a house again with a back yard was such a pleasure, since we were used to that most of our lives.

And for what it seemed, he and my friend had hit it off quite well. The very first time the U-HAUL truck stopped in front of his house and we entered inside with hand full of boxes, we came upon a quite peculiar situation. Our uncle was sitting in front of an active game of chess, all by himself. We figured whomever he was playing with will pop out of the bathroom momentarily. As we made several trips back and forth to the truck we realized he was playing by himself! My friend felt so bad for him, that after emptying most of the load he offered our uncle for a game of chess. I had never seen that man so happy and alive even though my friend beat him several times. My great uncle practically insisted that his challenger come over again. My friend happily accepted and sure enough those chess games became the reason why we became almost inseparable. The very thing I was so afraid of happening to me at such a young age, happened! I was getting engaged. Oh God, what can I say! Our home would come so alive and energized the minute he walked in through those doors and he was so respectful with my grandma and mom that part of me convinced myself that

73

getting engaged was the right thing to do. Deep down I knew it was the wrong thing for all the right reasons. I was not brought to this country to get married so fast and not even have the chance to pursue the happiness of this great land. Yet, I did not expect, nor foresee, my father dying on us and me growing up so fast either.

My soon to be fiancé filled such an emotional hole inside me that despite knowing clearly that marriage was not the answer, I was going to do it anyways.

The people who get on in this world are the people who get up and look for the circumstances they want, and, if they can't find them, make them.

GEORGE BERNARD SHAW, PLAYWRIGHT

CHAPTER 28

COMMUNISM IS EVIL / PURE AND SIMPLE

For most part, life for all of us was beginning to have some purpose, at least from my perspective. I was working harder then ever and saving to the maximum of my financial capability. In fact, I was hopeful; an automobile purchase was within my reach, maybe, just maybe, even an old Pontiac Trans Am or a Camaro. I was entitled to dream, right? Ever since our arrival into the free world I was doing a lot of that, dreaming that is. I strongly believed I was given that right the moment I stepped on the "land of the free". And no one, I mean not a single soul was ever going to convince me otherwise! One major component that was missing in my dreams, was comprehending the importance of education in this country through a mentor. Sure I could have gone to the school's counselor, yet I had known the purpose of the counselor's position. Restriction on my limited English speaking skills certainly did not help. Subconsciously I compared lifestyle here versus where I came from, all the time.

For example, let's take education, the one most important component in all humanity. Where we came from, there were hardly any dropouts. It certainly did not translate to all of us being hard working geniuses. Government had a legal way for fourteen year olds dropping out of school. The system was to graduate eighth grade and attend trade schools to become a blue collar society in the Soviet system. Not a problem there, right? That was the communistic mantra. So I got that. The bigger question was about all those who wanted to continue their education and even the bigger question WHY and HOW? As far as I was concerned my family barely earned enough money to feed us. Without bribery funds to the educators in charge, almost nobody got accepted to a university, Period. Almost everyone cheated and that was how the regimen operated. I was not going to dream nor had the intention to do so, because the outcome was crystal clear. Communism is a carefully calculated control on humanity.

I successfully purchased my first automobile with the help of my fiancé. No, not financially. I paid for that beauty all by myself; every penny of it was earned through hard work and dedication. That is why I felt so accomplished! And most importantly, it was my dream car, with my own earnings. A navy blue Trans Am with the proud eagle beautifully painted with its open wings spread on the hood. To me it represented freedom.

Our lives are sum total of the choices we have made.

WAYNE DYER

CHAPTER 29

MY OLDEST SISTER MARRIES A MUSLIM

On my nineteenth birthday, which was the second anniversary of my father's death, we all were headed to church, to the cemetery with a smaller group to follow with a luncheon in our backyard. My mother's sadness was unavoidable this year not so much the visit to the cemetery but due to my oldest sister wanting to get married to our neighbor from the apartment in Hollywood, whom she apparently kept contact with. The major objection was him being a Muslim man from Palestine. He was here on a student visa without any family. The reaction would have been the same if she was marrying a Jewish man from Israel or a black fellow from Africa. The concept of a young Armenian woman marrying outside our race, and particularly non Christian religion, was unfamiliar and forbidden! They were day and night different. I will never know the reason why she wanted to marry him. The logical answer for me was that she was in her late twenties and her time was running out, maybe? My grandma was all quiet about this sensitive issue, but the answer was clearly on her wise, wrinkled yet once beautiful facial feature. My mom was a different story! Constant argument arose about it. We did not communicate well generally and I figured what was the point of me giving her my two cents, from what I could tell she was going to marry him anyway! My middle sister was smart and neutral on the subject as well.

They were simply going to elope in the sin city and wanted me and my soon to be fiancé to be there for them. I agreed to be supportive yet my inner energy was very negative about this union. I could not shake that sixth sense out of me. I was very angry at myself for feeling the way I did.

My mom eventually wised up or got tired of the issue and came down from her high horse about the whole thing, realizing her inability to undo this upcoming marriage. We had a very small family gathering for the occasion with a couple of his friends.

For some reason I was on pins and needles in Las Vegas. It was so unfair to my sister the way I felt. She seemed to be in high spirits the whole trip and I wanted to be happy for her yet, I could not shake this unexplained inner feeling to the point where I was getting sick to my stomach.

The unwavering doubt about my forthcoming marriage was constantly haunting me and our first night spent together in a hotel room alone proved he was such a gentleman. Nothing inappropriate happened between the two of us. And no, I am not saying we just held hands all night, but he knew his limitations and felt my unspoken worries and insecurities. The bottom line is that he could have easily taken full advantage of a young vulnerable girl and he did not! The next morning I looked at him from a complete different angle. I wanted to scream from happiness to the world that I had the right guy by me at such a young age but did it really matter to anyone? Would anyone really believe me?

I should have been calm and free with my happiness but I could not. Deep inside my sixth sense was choking me to the point that I absolutely do not recall my sister's wedding ceremony. My brain and soul were too distraught to pay attention to the day's happenings. For some odd reason I just wanted to go home. Silently, I tried to shake this feeling off me but it was futile. So all day I secretly dealt with a racy heart and took deep breaths to try to keep myself calm!

Adversity and loss make a man wise.

WELSH PROVERB

CHAPTER 30

ANOTHER TRAGEDY!

We came across my grandma sitting by the dining table with my dad's cousin the moment we walked in through the side door of the house. I instantly sensed something was terribly wrong! I wanted more then anything to run from whatever was about to be said in that tiny dining room, so I mumbled something about being real tired and continued walking to the bathroom. Even this house was much bigger then the apartment we lived in previously, you could clearly hear normal conversations from different parts of the house. My escape was unsuccessful. As I sat on the toilet seat I heard part of the sentence about my mom being badly hurt in a car accident. I believe my body went into shock and my thinking got foggy. I kept thinking to myself she does not drive, how can she be in a car accident? I tried convincing myself that I must have heard it wrong. The conversation must be about someone else. And the minute I was able to walk, it would be clarified to me that nothing happened to my mom. At the same time I wanted to scream and cry and collapse onto the bathroom floor, but I could not move. I do remember instantly covering my ears with both hands real hard, because I did not want to know the rest. I discovered later in life about the human brain's incredible capacity to survive even during crises. My body was completely frozen like the arctic ice, yet my brain was jumping from one horror thought to the next. More then anything I wanted someone, anyone, to tell me that everything was going to be OK, that she was going to be just fine. But there was this eerie silence that was unbearable while we headed to the hospital and there was no one to tell me what I wanted to hear. My middle sister greeted us in the hallway of the hospital and before I could get the critical question out of my mouth both my sisters were hugging each other and hysterically crying in each other's arms. I was momentarily forgotten on the sidelines. I wanted to run to them and be hugged and let it all out of me, but of course once again I could not move. So I handled it the only way I knew how to, silently.

The future comes one day
at a time.

DEAN ACHESON

CHAPTER 31

THIS CAN'T BE HAPPENING!

Our middle sister explained us that according to the doctor, the first forty-eight hours were critical to her survival. While jay walking, she was hit by an oncoming automobile on a major Avenue, almost across the street from where we lived. Apparently the driver on the left lane, which was a van, made a complete stop, blocking the view of the driver on the right, unaware of a crossing pedestrian. She was hit and air thrown on to the curb with a major trauma to her head. She had broken body parts and black and purple covered her body as well, but the doctor's concentration was mainly on her head injuries. Numb and still in shock I returned home about midnight. My grandma and middle sister were in an argument, something about the fact that my grandma was alone at home when she heard the sirens and decided to come outside after a short while to see what was the commotion all about and found my mom's unconscious body on the curb. I felt incredibly sorry for my grandma, even more so than my mom for a moment. I even got angry with my mom for not using the crosswalk. But then again we were from a country where everything was just done like that. We just did not use crosswalks.

Visualizing the scene my grandma had described was in my worst nightmares for the longest time.

Don't be afraid to give your best at what seemingly are small jobs. Every time you conquer one it makes you that much stronger. If you do the little jobs well, the big ones will tend to take care of themselves.

DALE CARNEGIE

CHAPTER 32

BECOMING A BANKER BY SHEER LUCK

My mom was not a shy person; in fact, she was very personable. As far as I could remember, she thrived in helping others every possible way and sure enough her character did not stop in a new country, even with limited resources. She kept in contact with all of our neighbors from Armenia and some going all the way to Greece, distant relatives and old acquaintances who had immigrated to the United States in the seventies.

Since I was going to get married soon and start my own family I wanted to look for Monday through Friday jobs, hopefully eight to five. I tried the local papers for a short while and landed a couple of interviews. I knew they went horrible, due to my shyness and insecurities. My mom was going through her phone book and asking everyone if any of their kids, who worked at the local banks, would know of any job openings for me (all of this was taking place before the accident). I thought she was being ridiculous, (don't even know why), but I certainly could not have stopped her from making those calls. I was convinced nothing was going to come out of it. Well I was wrong! Surprisingly a lot of immigrant young people had landed professional jobs in few short years of being in this country. That was very impressive to me, I just did not think nor did not know how to get one. Well, my mother had it all arranged for me! She scheduled an appointment for me to meet up with one of our family friend's grandson, who happened to be working at the good old Security Pacific Bank. Within a few days I was called to an interview and it even went further than that and I was sent for a certain basic skills testing. Nervousness had set deep into the core of my gut and nothing made sense to me, to the point where my hands were like frozen ice and my eyes blurry. After for what seemed eternity staring at the blank test papers, I decided to glance on to the paper of a young Hispanic gentleman who happened to be sitting right next to me and conveniently had his paper clearly visible. He could have been failing the exam completely for all

I knew. I was desperate, so I marked the exact blanks as he. Did it ever cross my mind that I was cheating? Absolutely not! Don't mean to repeat myself over and over again, but where I came from it was the norm. I must have chosen my seat well, next to an intelligent person, because I was hired!

If the world seems cold to you, kindle fire to warm it.

LUCY LARCOM, HYMNIST

CHAPTER 33

HOME NOT SO SWEET

A new job awaited me, yet nervousness had paralyzed my soul. Between starting the job and for what seemed a catastrophe at home, breathing was becoming real difficult and hiding it was even more so. Deep inside these horrible thoughts haunted me. As horrifying as a new banking job seemed to me, I needed it more than ever to keep my mind busy and to retain my sanity, and above all stay away from home. Somehow, I pretended that everything was just fine, when I left the house. My mom would be home, awaiting my arrival from work, dinner ready on the table and as always something very fattening and tasty, what is now known to me as comfort food! Knowingly I would ignore my brain screaming loudly not to eat it and concentration would be on my empty and growling stomach. Oh and at that moment nothing mattered! The comfort food felt so good, that for few short minutes (I basically stuffed the food into my system) life felt good. Unfortunately the feel good moments were short lived and would disappear, leaving me with even lower self confidence, if it was at all possible. The one and only unwavering thought was always certain to me, being in this great Country was the best thing that ever happened to me.

And then the day came,
when the risk to remain tight
in a bud was more painful
than the risk it took
to blossom.

ANAIS NIN, DANISH DIARIST

CHAPTER 34

ANOTHER NEW WORLD FOR ME

English language seemed to have gotten easier to communicate with, until the first day at the bank. Survival was the key, during the two hour orientation, followed by an introduction to many, many people. Too many if you had asked me! Apparently this banking office was one of the main locations with training facilities on the second floor.

This was the near end for the good old times for the bankers, with ten a.m. to three p.m. operating hours with weekend offs. Thank goodness my training was assigned to the gentleman who had referred me. My survival at this job depended on my understanding skills (I mean the English language, that is). This was the first time I was in an English speaking professional environment. Fatigue had taken over my body at the end of the work day and it continued for several more days. And you know what, I was kind of glad, because I would be too tired to think and worry about the situation at home. My middle sister had taken it upon herself to take care of my mom and deal with the doctors with some help from my older sister. I was very happy about that as well. At this point, I would have gladly worked twenty four seven and take the financial responsibility side of things and not deal with anything else that I simply wanted to escape from.

Shut out all of your past
except that which will
help you weather your
tomorrows.

WILLIAM OSLER, CANADIAN PHYSICIAN

CHAPTER 35

GOOD PEOPLE ARE EVERYWHERE

Prognosis on my mom's health was grim. On the positive note she had survived this horrific accident (thank heavens a million times); however, the damage to her brain was so severe that it was going to take many months, if not years, for her memory and senses to be back to normal. At this point in my life I had lost my individuality and any self esteem that I had. Sadly, I had forgotten my sweet grandma's silky strokes with her severe arthritic yet once beautiful hands. I honestly was wrapped up in my own world and did not know from one day to the next. To even consider talking about my emotional status with my fiancé or anybody else was unthinkable, so I thought! What I loved about him was his high energy that he seemed to always have. It did perk me up a little at least on the surface, temporarily! During this chapter of my life I found some support from the least expected place of all. At the lunch room of my workplace, where a bunch of ladies of all different ethnicity and ages. Let's see, a Cuban, an Italian, Jamaican, Lebanese, couple of Caucasians and a semi-retired Armenian lady (did not speak any Armenian) as young as in their late twenties to as old as late sixties, would gather around a table and talk about everyday life. During the first few weeks I typically was passive and would listen. They all certainly tried to get me involved; especially a couple of the older women who kind of took me under their wing, so to speak. It felt good to be in their company. I certainly did not discuss my family situation. I kept the personal information at minimal. It was too painful to say out loud that my father had died recently on my birthday and my mom hardly recognizes me due to a brain injury, on top of our uncertain financial situation. Tears would pop out of those tiny holes in the corner of my eyes and the battle would begin to force them back unsuccessfully.

If others believe in you, you also eventually believe in yourself Keep away from the people who try to belittle your ambitions. Small people always do that, but the really great ones make you feel that you, too, can become great.

MARK TWAIN, WRITER AND SATIRIST

There was a lot for me to learn and absorb. It seemed like most everyone around me cared for my success. Computer era was at its baby steps, so everything was manually processed, and there were lots and lots of detailed handwritten work for me to comprehend. The gentleman who was in charge of my training was a calm and patient individual and I was eternally grateful to him, yet his silence made me doubt myself constantly. It was these ladies who gave me motherly pats on the shoulder and their expressions gave me the reassurance. Those memorable lunch hours became the focus of my days (and I don't mean the eating part). It was like therapy and a crash course in American history. These ladies were amazing. I knew instantly what had really attracted me to this group. There was a high moral ground amongst them that I found fascinating! And another real important thing I learned from them was that reasonable people were equal, regardless of race, color, height, weight and everything else that pertained to humanity! An average human being has the same dreams for themselves and their families, and if anywhere in the world there is a possibility to make them a reality, that would be in the great country of the United States of America. Yes, I firmly, undoubtedly believed this. You know what, that thought was always in the back of my uneasy mind and gave me comfort to tap into that thought from time to time. Before long I was mastering the skills of good old banking and my environment had done wonders for my English speaking skills, to the point where I was the master trainer for new hires that were trained at our main office. Imagine that!

The value of marriage is not that adults produce children but that children produce adults.

PETER DE VRIES, NOVELIST AND EDITOR

CHAPTER 36

MIRACLE OF SURVIVING TEENAGE MARRIAGE

October 6th was marked on the calendar as my wedding day. I did not fully comprehend the seriousness of that day, but then again I was a nineteen year old teenager with many unresolved sad issues in my life. Marriage was my escape route and I dammed well knew it, I simply would ignore my strong intuition and wanted so desperately to fix things for my family to the highest of my capability. My attraction/love (if I can include the word Love in this sentence) for my fiancé was very real, as real as it can be for a teenager AND lots of immigrant girls my age were getting married and making their families very happy by producing next generation babies, before their first anniversary. Well, I was not going to be any different nor did I want to be at this point. We already know how both grandma and mom felt about my oldest sister's taste in marriage. Majority of my middle sister's time was consumed by taking care of my mom and school. All of this was justified for me to get married. My fiancé truly believed we were ready for this marriage business (the fact of the matter was, that was the only way for us to be together). More then anything I wanted to believe that. Most of the time I convinced myself that it was so.

Obviously there was not going to be a whole lot of planning for our big day. There would be a church ceremony, of course, and I would be dressed in a white wedding gown, which was borrowed from family. That would be just about it. That was just fine with me. Honestly! We had many other issues to deal with, like where and how we were going to reside and make a living. Monetary necessity was unavoidable, regardless of the size of our wedding. Without hesitation I decided to sell the Trans Am. The tragedies in the last couple of years had sculpted me to always prepare for the unexpected, unfortunately always with the anticipation of the worst on my part. What helped me to carry through life was the upbeat and positive personality of my future husband. He sometimes came across as arrogant but he always backed his claims through hard work. In fact, he is one of the hardest working individuals I came to know with type "A" personality. He will not stop until he accomplishes whatever he has his mind on, until the next project he brings on with full blown enthusiasm. I mean this guy does not stop.

Having written all of the above, did we have marital issues? Of course! We were kids and there was so much growing up to happen between the both of us and I say if we did not have sooooo much interference from the family, life would have been a bit easier! However, this book is not about my marriage. I believe that would be a whole different book titled the title of this chapter "Miracle of surviving teenage marriage."

Without forgiveness life is governed by…an endless cycle of resentment and retaliation.

ROBERT ASSAGIOLO

CHAPTER 37

NOT SO FREE IN THE FREE WORLD

So the Trans Am was on sale. Only for a brief moment I would allow myself to miss that beauty that I had been so determined to have. In some ways I had grown beyond my years and really had comprehended the insignificance of material goods. If nothing else, the purchase of the automobile had been a confidence booster on my capabilities, and once again I clearly knew the possibilities in this great free nation were limitless.

It was customary, and in some cases mandatory by the groom's parents, for newlyweds to live with the family, so when my future mother-in-law told us that we did not have to live with them I was honestly ecstatic for obvious reasons. I more than anything wanted to create a peaceful and private life for me and my husband. Wanting to start something fresh, with the hopes of erasing all bad, which had happened to us, pretty much upon our arrival to the States. The scars were deep like a horrendous tornado that ran deep down my veins. Let's be realistic, what reasonable bride to be would not want to start a new family without the extended family members in one's face. My dreams of creating my own life and place were short-lived, when my soon to be husband dropped the bomb at me announcing that he had this genius idea of both of us and his family buying a house together instead of paying two separate rents. It would not even occur to him that the subject needed to be open for discussion. One thing I am certain of, is that my disapproval was clearly visible, though with unspoken words. Although his family did raise questions about his plan. Financially it was a great idea, especially for an immigrant family, not so brilliant in any other aspect. Before long we had an agent (of course an Armenian) who was showing us properties. I have to admit that the idea of living in a house with a back yard was very appealing. Like a little child within days I was up in arms ready for the adventure of house hunting and it did not even matter that the whole family was going to live together. If you have seen the movie / comedy "The Greek Wedding", we Armenians are no different, except real life is no comedy.

Know your limits…but never stop trying to exceed them.

ANONYMOUS

CHAPTER 38

TAPPING AT AMERICAN DREAM

Clueless and unaffected by the economic situation of the early 80's there was a whole new world for us to comprehend from the purchase of the house to a loan qualification. All of this "credit" business was foreign to us. The "familiar" to us was to get paid, cash the check and pay for basic necessities, only after the rent was met. Naturally we bombarded the poor agent with endless questions. He seemed like a reasonable guy and patiently answered and in most cases detailed the answers. The more we got educated on real estate and what was involved for a purchase, unlike my fiancé, my attitude along with his family was pessimistic. He of course did not want to hear any of the complaints nor the concerns.

The abandoned major fixer that we stumbled upon in the San Fernando Valley area, with a good vision and endless hours, days and months of work would become a welcoming home for anyone who stuck around my fiancé long enough. His vibrant energy was certainly contagious. On the reality side of things, the asking price for this anticipated beauty was little over one hundred thousand dollars. WOW! That was seriously an intimidating amount of DOLLARS for us. Apparently out of desperation to sell the property, the owner would carry a second on the house between fifteen to twenty thousand dollars at a whooping ten percent interest rate, annually. All we had to do, come up with about that much between the six of us for down payment, which would be both of us, my parent- in-laws, his grandmother and sister.

I am a great believer in luck,
and I find the harder I work,
the more I have of it.

THOMAS JEFFERSON, PRESIDENT AND PHILOSOPHER

CHAPTER 39

ENDLESS POSSIBILITIES

For what seemed an endless and intimidating process, within weeks of our wedding day we were handed the key of our own home! This was happening to an immigrant family, only after a handful of years residing in this country. For god's sake we were nowhere close to mastering the English language, yet we almost owned our own property! Does the reader comprehend the power behind this purchase? Most people in the entire world do not get the opportunity to own their piece of land in their countries, and if you live under communism you are forbidden to own almost anything of your own! Sadly it is mostly government controlled. So this was huge for us. Sure it was made possible by all six of us working hard and many sacrifices, but then again, globally millions of people's hard work barely gets them basic food if lucky enough, let alone their own property.

With the electrified leadership of my husband all of us rolled up our sleeves and almost immediately went to work. Endless hours and days were spent on clearing several layers of wallpaper from every single wall of the house to breaking down wired actual chicken sheds in the back yard. Even with twenty four seven constant effort we could not complete the project before our big day. The fact that we could not complete the project was killing my fiancé despite us (he myself and his sister) staying up into the wee hours for several nights and basically collapsing on the floor on a cold autumn night. He will never admit this, but on a few days getaway on our honeymoon, at times his mind was very preoccupied with the incomplete project. I thought we balanced each other quite well with my calm and his hyper personalities.

I am a kind of paranoiac
in reverse.
I suspect people of plotting
to make me happy.

JD SALINGER

CHAPTER 40

TRADITIONS

Can't tell you how relieved I was to have been done and finished with the day of the wedding. It should have been the happiest day of my life; sadly it was not, due to any attention I despised so much. I truly believed I did not deserve any. As far as I could remember, I was teased, criticized or ignored (being ignored was the better choice). The attention I received was mainly negative and had something to do with my weight. The truth of the matter was, there was no one I would go to for comfort or protection. So to be married, meant to belong to someone, who would swim through shark infested waters for one, the way Dr. Laura Schlesinger (I listened to her on a radio program in later years) puts it. (I was convinced I had married that person). He gave me what I craved so desperately, except life is not as simple as I had anticipated. To complicate things a bit more, all one has to do is to get pregnant as young as we were, and that is exactly what happened to me due to complete ignorance. Once again, I so badly wanted to go "with the flow" and "fix" things for my family that I thought this child would bring happiness, especially to my beloved grandmother. I did not know the first thing about raising a child, nor were we anyway ready for this addition at this point in our lives. I clearly, way deep down knew that my actions were for all the wrong reasons, but it was too easy to ignore my instincts and just go with the flow!

I did not think morning sickness was all that terrible, figuring that since it was part of the pregnancy I had to accept and deal with it. The baby was coming mid summer and the heat was becoming almost unbearable (of course we did not have the luxury of air conditioning). Where we came from we did not even know about the existence of air conditioning, among many other things, and that notion helped a lot to accept just about anything. I had figured this much, complaining certainly was not going to help, so with a little patience and discipline I could talk myself into believing that it really was not so bad. I did literally talk to myself, actually a lot. It was sort of calming to me, like therapy. Anything of my concern would turn into a two way conversation in my head.

Even though the answers came from me, somehow were satisfactory. If I could brag for myself a moment (the way interviewers ask that last question, what are your best and worst qualities?) My innocence was my savior. Anyone who would smile at me I was ready to give my whole and some, and the ones who did not I avoided any confrontation at all cost. I was not equipped or adult enough to know how to confront anyone without a racy heart and sweaty palms, yet I was having a child.

No change of
circumstances can repair a
defect of character.

RALPH WALDO EMERSON, WRITER

CHAPTER 41

EMBRACING NEW TRADITIONS

Surprise is an understatement, truly, when the entire work force gave me the most amazing and unfamiliar party called a baby shower! The roomy lunch area was transformed into a tastefully decorated party room with pastel colored balloons and baby stuff. The gifts were amazing. One of the ladies from work held a second job at Bullocks department store and had offered her employee discount for the purchasing of the baby items. All of this was for me and the baby? Such beautiful and much needed items and so much of it! I was speechless and once again, very uncomfortable with all the attention. Who was I to deserve all this? Apparently all these people thought I was worthy of it, except myself. I don't think they knew how much their generosity meant to me and I did not know how to show proper appreciation besides the many verbal thanks. The same lady with the Bullock's discount brought this issue to my attention with a little attitude, completely unaware of my ignorance in this area. First and foremost I was ashamed beyond words, and decided to come out the only way I knew, honestly, and explain to her that where I came from there were no such things as thank you cards or notes but promised myself and her that I would write a thank you note for every opportunity I was given. I am forever grateful for the lady's boldness to have taught me a very important lesson. One of the many joys in my life is to write sincere notes and thank everyone for their kindness or gift or time or simply for being good humans.

The first sign of a nervous breakdown is when you start thinking your work is terribly important.

MILO BLOOM

CHAPTER 42

MOTHERHOOD

My first experience of true happiness was the actual birth of my son. If I did not believe in miracles, the experience changed all of that and left me speechless. Unfortunately the moment had passed too quickly and realities and responsibilities were a little too harsh for a teenager my age. One of the problems was how to be myself. There were too many of us under one roof, loving and raising this bundle of joy. To make matters worse, I had to go back to work within six weeks. I would have more then anything given up everything to raise my child, not that I had anything to give up, but the realities of life had different plans for our future. The loving union of big family barely lasted a year and we smart adults deserted this child even further. My husband and I with our little boy moved out of this dream house of ours and now had him under a babysitter's care. That stood against everything I believed in! I am afraid even Dr. Laura could not have helped me due to my insecurities and vulnerabilities at the time. I know now that we did what was familiar and how we were raised. We did provide food and clothing and home, yet not enough time was spent with him at the park or strolls by the beach or anything in that nature, not even close to giving enough time! I strongly believe it is irresponsible to bring a precious child into this world and not be available to raise him or her. In my opinion, that defines of providing them with loving and a caring set of married parents (yes, to each other) spending time with them the moment they enter this world, discipline them, teach them, read to and with them, love them some more and spend precious time doing silly things free of care, laugh a lot, hug a lot and love them some more and more, and one day to see the colorful and firm fruit of your hard yet most rewarding labor on this planet. One can always argue that most of us turned out to be all right not given most of the above, and that is the farthest from the truth. Of course this is my strong opinion about parenting and, yes, in my mind I was ignorant and guilty of most of the above under the circumstances life had thrown at me.

Even if our efforts of attention seem for years to be producing no result, one day a light that is in exact proportion to them will flood the soul.

SIMONE WEIL

CHAPTER 43

WISDOM COMES WITH AGE

If reruns were possible in real life I would erase most of my twenties and start all over again, just like it is done during a movie shoot. Pretty strong statement, but that's the truth, so help me God. Since the above was impossible, I was going to make that part of my life my long educational period. Absolutely no blame on anyone. Oh, what would I have done to have the never ending growing wisdom that I have now! Aging, good reads and few wise men (and of course a real wise woman) have become priceless figures in my life. These wise people that I am talking about became parents and mentors. Listening to these folks via radio and television empowered me, though it was through very baby steps. It was almost like slowly waking up from a coma! I wasn't just a care giver any longer to my family. I actually was questioning things in life. Political conversations sparked flames in my soul. I certainly was quite ignorant in the political arena as well to actually carry on an intelligent conversation with anyone, and my simple mind was starving for the knowledge. I wanted more than anything to learn American Politics. After all, the entire world, OK maybe that is an exaggeration, but most of the world population wanted to be part of the "land of the free" that was only two hundred some years old? Why so? Was it under the generosity of the American Constitution or the freedoms of the ordinary people making extraordinary lives for their families through self relied opportunities? My mind would be overwhelmed with all sorts of questions. So I decided to begin my quest with co-workers, since that was my only American contact. These conversations would mostly take place in the lunch room area, during lunch hour. Lucky for me I discovered that most Americans are friendly and giving individuals. They were more than willing to share their thoughts and experiences about this country. I had seen political conversations turn into full blown arguments or yell outs, so I was very cautious and disciplined about the topic. I generally was the listening party, and for a good reason. Of course, silently my mind would be made up (just like in my childhood) The interfiling was satisfactory.

....

There are two kinds of man:
the ones who make history
and the ones who endure it.

CAMILO JOSE CELA, SPANISH NOVELIST

....

CHAPTER 44

THE FACTOR EFFECT

Trying to walk off my weight, I decided to invest in a treadmill. With my husband's help we acquired an inexpensive and noisy machine (with my insistence that it be the least expensive) from the local Wal-Mart store. It was naturally set up in front of the television tube at a reasonable distance for my daily power walks. I would have loved to read while on the treadmill, unsuccessfully. Sitcoms and game shows were becoming plain old boring. I was very uninterested playing with the remote control while exercising, and sixty minutes were becoming real drags. A good amount of money was invested in this machine, so stopping the power walks was out of the question. I just had to find a good program that would grab enough of my interest to keep me on the darn machine for an hour and I found the task quite challenging, until one amazing day, I stumbled upon this program on the Fox cable channel called the O'Reilly Factor. My jaw dropped within the first few minutes of listening to this guy. There was so much passion in his voice that my sixty minute workouts flew by! That alone for me was a miracle! Could a political television program have this kind of effect on me? It was like a juicy soap opera that I had seen a bunch of women at work get hooked, except this was better, much, much better, at least for me. I had not felt this intelligent for as long as I was alive. Before long The Factor program, my treadmill and I, became hooked. Boy, was I starved of political information and any history about this country was fascinating to me, and how Mr. O presented it made all the difference. It was simplified for a simple individual like myself. My discovery of The Factor program was too exiting not to share with others, so very naively in a conversation, I mentioned it to a friend. To my utter surprise, O'Reilly was a very controversial man! I patiently let her get it out of her system whatever it was that she had an issue with. She simply did not make any sense, and I knew I had matured by letting her finish her argument. I started laughing and my laughter got her confused, because I had only mentioned his name. Very politely I got her permission to speak and that confused her further. When I was able to speak, she got an invitation from me to my home to share a meal and watch The Factor and then we could discuss the program. I also asked this mature woman the last time she had watched The Factor. Her honesty was very much appreciated. She said "oh it's been a while". She never came to my house, but little old immigrant me scored big with her after discussing few general areas, such as single parenting and drugs. As a matter of fact, she was a third generation Irish woman, who is old enough to be my mother. Our conversation ended with her saying "I guess I am more of a traditional woman than I thought".

Try to learn to breathe deeply, really to taste food when you eat and when you sleep really to sleep. Try as much as possible to be wholly alive with all your might, and when you laugh, laugh like hell.

WILLIAM SAROYAN, DRAMATIST AND AUTHOR

CHAPTER 45

MATURITY COMES WITH AGE (FOR MOST)

So many tragedies in my young life had humbled me deep down to the core. It was either faith or energy, or both, that good people came my way. One of the special individuals who did just that and literally began raising me in my early thirties (something very unfamiliar to me) through her radio program was the one and only infamous Dr. Laura Schlesinger. This tough yet genuine woman was the answer to my prayers, and before long my lunch hours were spent in my car turning into priceless therapy sessions. Time did not permit the full benefits of this magnificent program, amazingly the impact it implied on my life, continuing to this very day. Dr. Laura would be so proud of her angelic work on me. Over time, I watched myself become a secure and confident mother and wife! She made me cry, sob and laugh out loud, that turned into more tears many times. God only knows how many thousands of times I profusely have thanked her for the transformation in my head. Between Dr. Laura, Bill O'Reilly, my son's Christian school's bible teachings and many other great characters that have touched me so deeply, life had certainly become a lot more meaningful and the bad were just moments. Almost three decades of my life has passed, like the gentle breeze that sometime has turned into full blown gust with dark sand in it and at times it has almost swept me off balance and again and again I have recovered, each time just a bit stronger and always grateful for the opportunity that came from complete strangers.

For both myself and my mother's sake I wanted to have as close of a relationship as possible and the connection were my kids. Thankfully she spent real quality time with them, reading (in Armenian), telling bedtime stories, drawing pictures, playing cards to name a few. Her accident had visible marks on her health. Of course her poor diet and lifestyle did not help the situation. To clarify her "lifestyle", she did not smoke or drink or had the finances to dine out or anything as such. She simply did not take care of herself as far as her diet and exercise, nor did she know or want to. I liberally criticized her on the subject due to her constant complaints and that never set well between us. Her daily complaints via telephone or in person had become a real drag. The sadness, her complaints were very legitimate, yet the consistency of them robbed her of the seriousness of her condition. And when she and I were able to have "normal" conversations, which was a rare occasion, there were so many unanswered questions about her helplessness, beginning as basic yet crucial to ones survival as not speaking the English Language that was spoken in this country and so many thousands more like tens of thousands of other immigrants alike, completely at the financial mercy of this government (not wanting to recognize nor acknowledge that the so called government is the "people"). Yes, the very Americans, that got called names by the immigrants that I was surrounded sometimes. For what it seemed, the world was pouring into the United States of America. In mind, constantly came Dr. Martin Luther King's famous quote "I have a dream". I consider myself a simple individual and thought my dream was as simple as it can be. Such a simple dream, yet, I could not for the life of me have many understand or accept the concept of self reliance. I would be forever grateful to my mom for the difficult, yet very important decision she had made many years ago to move us to this great land. I just wanted her and many in her position to understand the concept behind the government's programs.

The man who wants to lead
the orchestra must turn his
back on the crowd.

JAMES CROOK

CHAPTER 46

FORBIDDEN TOPIC

My simple dream and the question of self reliance had brought tons of turmoil my direction, during simple dinner gatherings with family and friends, which we had plenty of at our home. No need to wait for Christmas or major holiday to get together was my husband's philosophy on the subject. Honestly, I enjoyed it myself, for the most part. Since we were part of the earlier group of immigrants, we took it upon ourselves to make it our moral obligation to look out for the newcomers, whether it be an ex neighbor, relatives or at times complete strangers, who had no one close enough to pick them up from the airport. Due to my somewhat fluent English speaking skills, my social services were volunteered to the newcomers, like the Gas Company's slogan (glad to be of service) beginning first and foremost a visit to the local Social Security office, followed by the welfare offices and so on and so forth. Just about every immigrant family had two to three kids, which qualified them for welfare program and a senior adult family member or two, automatically qualified for Social Security Program, the American citizens contribute throughout their working lives. Just a little crash course on the amendment by President Jimmy Carter on the Social Security program in the seventies. He signed it into law, anyone immigrating to the United States at the age of 65 years or older to automatically qualify for the benefits, without contributing a dime to the fund! Genius, wasn't he? (NOT) Such a disservice to the American Taxpayer!

Part of me was very proud to help these helpless immigrants settle, in an effort of pursuing the American Dream, thus a stronger part of me cringed at the thought of these people living off the American taxpayer, knowing full well that for some, it would become a lifestyle.

Watching my kids enjoy their time with our guests was very fulfilling. The gatherings got interesting and intense at times, along with my undivided attention, when and if any negative conversation revolved around this great country and its people. Surrounded by newly arrived immigrants, the political conversations were almost inevitable. It was almost unexplained passion that took over me during these times. If I can characterize my behavior it was similar to a frantic mother protecting its child from great danger. My heart pounding clearly in my ears, like loud drums playing nearby, to a point where I would experience cold and shaky hands. But what was killing me more, was my own silence. Surely something had to be said and fast. "Lisa breathe and breathe some more" is what an inner voice would demand of me, knowing real well the outcome of the conversation I was about to engage in. Calmly yet passionately I would do so while almost always having a mental thought of my mentor, Dr. Laura and later in years Bill O'Reilly. Sadly, the first "looks" would come my direction from my husband, and as much as I wanted or was expected to be the obedient wife, my passion would take over, failing my wifely duties. He would much rather I keep my thoughts to myself, knowing full well that the majority of our company would kind of agree with each other. My answer always "I rather be dead than not speak my opinion on simple logic". What will remain a mystery to me is the hypocrisy of some immigrants, who could not wait to get out of the former Soviet regimen. United States did not invite them to move to this country; the immigrants voluntarily and very patiently (did not have much of a choice) stood in the communist regimes long and painful lines for months and most of the time, years (detailed in earlier chapter) to come to the free world. This is not something I heard from someone. I was there, as you know, and my memory is crystal clear! Sadly, much had changed from the immigrant's point of views, who came in the beginning of the twentieth century to become Americans!

I am not a politician. I am an ordinary citizen with a deep-seated belief that much of what troubles us has been brought about by politicians.

RONALD REAGAN, REAGAN FOR GOVERNOR OF CALIFORNIA

CHAPTER 47

WHAT HAPPENED TO HUMAN DIGNITY?

Due to my unwavering love for this great land, I want to emphasize on the immigration issue and put forth my take on the subject. My passion is to such extent, that the issue deserves a long chapter of honest and painful facts. For God's sake, who better then I would know the details of this controversial topic. It seems only few years ago we were on the same mission, though it has been a lot longer. In my true humble opinion, this delicate topic is crucial for the financial recovery and above all, safety of this Great Nation and its hard working people. The Federal Government has decided to completely wash their hands of this topic, strictly for political reason. What a shame! Shouldn't the governments' first and foremost obligation be to its citizens? After all it is those very people, whose hard earned dollars are supporting this unmatched system. Yet, over the years this unresolved issue has gotten so out of control, that some patriotic citizens have taken the protection of this great country into their own hands by risking their lives. Our laws very graciously entitle an immigrant family and or an individual, who legally moves to United States of America, to receive financial benefits at state and or federal levels in order to expedite the transition of settling. To simplify the above or be blunt, the immigrant(s) get paid taxpayer dollar in several different form of method, depending on age and marital status. I became an expert real fast on this subject, helping countless families with the process. One particular volunteer mission to the local Social Security office will forever stay in my mind. The reason for my availability to this large family during a weekday was strictly coincidental. I was very pregnant with my daughter and had stayed home, for being under the weather, until I was woken up by a phone call. I honestly did not know how to turn down anyone for help. I was in tears as I was putting on some clothes on my worn out body for not being able to say NO even with a real legitimate reason. Next thing, we were in the local Social Security Office and with every ounce of energy I was convincing myself that this would be over quickly. I could not have been more wrong about it. Apparently the immigration officials at the Los Angeles International Airport completely missed this family of six by a "minor" detail. They simply missed to attach the "white card" to their passports that makes their entrance to the country legal. Oops! The entire day was not enough! This was just the beginning of some of the agencies of the Government I would be chaperoning many families for the assistance they would require for the "pursuit of happiness" in the Greatest Nation in the entire Planet. Let's summarize this. This great nation open arms takes the legal immigrants and cradles them to their success, by providing low income housing, finances for their living, financial aid for education (adult and children), after school program for youngsters, day and healthcare services for the elderly and the list goes on and on and on. Apparently that is not enough by some politicians, and now in the last couple of decades all of the above is also available to the illegal immigrants! All of the financial help combined sums up to couple of thousand dollars per family, per month, more or less on an average. By American standards of living that is considered poor or below poverty levels, yet globally that is above middle class. So, for many, sadly this easily becomes a lifestyle. And if they work getting paid cash, then they become "financially comfortable". Throughout my life, reading has been my number one source of knowledge and information, but meeting and chatting with incredible knowledgeable Americans has been a great stimulant for my brain. The attached data will be an eye opener for the reader as it was for me, sent to me by one of my dear and smart American friend! Let me tell you something! This is NOT what the founding fathers envisioned some two hundred years ago!

It's easy to dismiss individual programs that benefit non-citizens until they're put together and this picture emerges. Someone did a lot of research to put together all of this data. Often these programs are buried within other programs making them difficult to find.

A Real Eye Opener ...

Why is the USA BANKRUPT?

Informative,and mind boggling!

You think the war in Iraq was costing us too much? Read this:

We have been hammered with the propaganda that it was the Iraq war and the war on terror that is bankrupting us.

I now find that to be RIDICULOUS.

I hope the following 14 reasons are read over and over again until they are read so many times that the reader gets sick of reading them. I also have included the URL's for verification of all the following facts...

1. $11 Billion to $22 billion is spent on welfare to illegal aliens each year by state governments. Verify at: http://www.fairus.org/site/PageServer?pagename=iic_immigrationissuecenters7fd8

2. $2.2 Billion dollars a year is spent on food assistance programs such as food stamps, WIC, and free school lunches for illegal aliens. Verify at: http://www.cis.org/articles/2004/fiscalexec.HTML

3. $2.5 Billion dollars a year is spent on Medicaid for illegal aliens. Verify at: http://www.cis.org/articles/2004/fiscalexec.HTML

4. $12 Billion dollars a year is spent on primary and secondary school education for children here illegally and they cannot speak a word of English! Verify at: http://transcripts.cnn.com/TRANscriptS/0604/01/ldt..0.HTML

5. $17 Billion dollars a year is spent for education for the American-born children of illegal aliens, known as anchor babies. Verify at http://transcripts.cnn.com/TRANscriptS/0604/01/ldt01.HTML

6. $3 Million Dollars a DAY is spent to incarcerate illegal aliens. Verify at: http://transcripts.cnn.com/%20TRANscriptS/0604/01/ldt.01. HTML

7. 30% percent of all Federal Prison inmates are illegal aliens Verify at: http://transcripts.CNN.com/TRANscriptS/0604/01/ldt.01.HTML cnn.com/TRANscriptS/0604/01/ldt.01.HTML%3E;

8. $90 Billion Dollars a year is spent on illegal aliens for Welfare & social services by the American taxpayers. Verify at: http://premium.cnn. com/TRANSCIPTS/0610/29/ldt.01.HTML

9. $200 Billion dollars a year in suppressed American wages are caused by the illegal aliens. Verify at: http://transcripts.cnn.com/TRANSC%20 RI%20PTS/0604/01/ldt.01.HTML

10. The illegal aliens in the United States have a crime rate that's two and a half times that of white non-illegal aliens. In particular, their children are going to make a huge additional crime problem in the US. Verify at: http://transcripts.cnn./.com/TRANscriptS/0606/12/ ldt..01.HTML

11. During the year of 2005 there were 4 to 10 MILLION illegal aliens that crossed our Southern Border also, as many as 19,500 illegal aliens from Terrorist Countries.. Millions of pounds of drugs, cocaine, meth, heroin and marijuana, crossed into the US from the Southern border. Verify at: Homeland Security Report:

12. The National policy Institute estimated that the total cost of mass deportation would be between $206 and $230 billion or an average cost of between $41 and $46 billion annually over a five year period. Verify at: http://www.nationalpolicyinstitute./.org/PDF/deportation. PDF

13. In 2006, illegal aliens sent home $45 BILLION in remittances to their countries of origin. Verify at: http://www/..rense.com/general75/ niht.htm

14. The Dark Side of Illegal Immigration: Nearly One million sex crimes Committed by Illegal Immigrants In The United States . Verify at: http: // www.drdsk.com/articleshtml < ww http: articleshtml%3E; www.drdsk.com>;%20w.drdsk.com/articleshtml

The total cost is a whopping $ 338.3 BILLION DOLLARS A YEAR AND IF YOU'RE LIKE ME, HAVING TROUBLE UNDERSTANDING THIS AMOUNT OF MONEY; IT IS $338,300,000,000.00 WHICH WOULD BE ENOUGH TO STIMULATE THE ECONOMY FOR THE CITIZENS OF THIS COUNTRY.

Are we THAT stupid? YES, FOR LETTING THOSE IN THE U.S. CONGRESS GET AWAY WITH LETTING THIS HAPPEN YEAR AFTER YEAR!!!!!

Franklin Roosevelt, a democrat, introduced the Social Security Program. He promised

That participation would be completely voluntary, no longer voluntary.

That the participants would only have to pay 1 percent of the first $1,400.00 of their annual income.

That the money the participants elected to put into the program would be deductible from their income for tax purposes each year, no longer deductible

That the money put into the "Trust Fund" would only be used to fund Social Security retirement program and under President Johnson (democrat) the money was moved to the general fund and spent.

That the annuity payments to the retirees would never be taxed as income. Under president Clinton up to 85 percent of Social Security was taxed.

After violating the original contract the democrats turn around and tell its citizens that the Republicans want to take the Social Security away and the worst part about it, is uninformed citizens believe it! On the other hand we never hear democrats scare the welfare recipients that the welfare program is running out of funds! Scary, isn't it?

To fulfill a dream, to be allowed to sweat over lonely labor, and to be given a chance to create, are the meat and potatoes of life. The money is the gravy.

BETTY DAVIS, ACTRESS

CHAPTER 48

WHERE DID TIME GO BY?

As much as I would have liked and dreamed for most immigrants to see and understand my point of view about this country and its possibilities, make this issue the center of my universe, even make a career out of it, I did not know how to pursue this dream or if I was even entitled to it! The reality of life and responsibilities always slapped me hard on both sides of my face and the ordinary always won. From time to time something deep from within screamed at me to act and the power of that moment is indescribable, yet time and time again I chose to ignore the screams or the ignorance of me took over. This is going to sound crazy, but when my mom's health showed many signs of deterioration I took a big sigh of relief for the distraction of my thoughts from my never ending passion without progress. I would have an excuse not to have the time!

I could not believe the misfortune of my family's destiny and it saddened me to the core to see her ill, knowing well that this time it was quite serious. Justification of my ordinary responsibilities with my daily duties to my family and now my mom's illness was a big fat lie to me. I knew in the two decades I had matured plenty, thanks to Dr. Laura.

More than anything I wanted to be there for my mom. And more than anything I knew there were bigger things in the horizon for me, only if I could reach and grab them.

In her sixty-eight years of life my mother had immigrated twice, at 14 and again at age 46. Her accomplishments were minimal. But I believe by producing children who can reach for those almost impossible stars (once again in the land of the opportunity), a nice chunk of the accomplishment must be credited to my parents. I finally figured it out that immigrating second time around; my parents gave up a lot for our lives to be better.

I had played with the book idea enough already and when my mom passed away only at 68 years of age, I knew I was ready to put our life story down on paper as an inspiration for every individual, whether immigrant or five generation American, especially young Americans! As much as I had matured, one thing that I hadn't learned nor wanted was to show my emotions. Control and discipline in most cases won. I still wanted so desperately to make things better or hoping that I could make a difference.

To be nobody but yourself in
a world which is doing
its best, night and day, to
make you everybody else,
means to fight the hardest
battle which any human
being can fight; and never
stop fighting.

ED CUMMINGS, POET

CHAPTER 49

KNOWLEDGE IS POWER

Over the years, reading, listening and watching every article and material accessible to me about health and fitness flew out the window in an instant after the death of my mother. The one comfortable and familiar place for me to turn to was the biggest enemy I fought my entire life, FOOD. And not just any, but the most damaging one, sugary sweets. Conveniently and unfortunately it seemed like it was all over my house, everywhere I turned. It is customary for Armenians to visit the deceased family with pastries, especially the first seven days, and it can continue for up to forty. Since I was the main caregiver for my mom in the later years of her life, all our relatives and her friends and neighbors visited my home (with boxes of the dangerous goodies). Armenian populated towns like Glendale, Burbank and parts of San Fernando Valley are filled with fresh bakeries that have some amazingly tasteful pastries. These little things worked on my emotional pain like the oxycodone (very strong medication for pain with prescription) on someone with severe pain! One is simply never enough! And then the "feel good" moment is gone and your misery is back with vengeance! Many nights I gladly gave up dinner to indulge in pastries that I had looked forward to the moment they entered my home, justifying to myself that I was eating pretty much the same amount of calories. Who was I kidding? You know what other crazy justification came to mind constantly? Oprah. I thought, my God, if this powerful woman can't control her weight issues with her money, who am I to even attempt at this battle, forgetting that I had done it and not only I had done it but money had not much to do with it". Something had to be done about this and fast, because I could only hide my misery for so long. I owed it to my family, to be a mentally and physically healthy mother and wife. As I was battling this transformational phase I heard a caller on Dr. Laura show conversing my issue. This was no accident, because I could only listen to less then an hour of her three hour program during my short lunch break. The moment I turned the car engine on, a sad voice came on asking Dr. Laura about my situation. I knew the answer all along, yet coming from this woman, whom I had so much respect for and had gotten helped in so many other areas of my life, it clicked. The pain I had was not going to magically go away, I had to slowly put it away by doing all the right things in my life, beginning with the elimination of stuffing my one and only body with sugary stuff. And you want to know something brutally honest about my pain; it was not about losing my mother as much, as about the numbness of it all.

When half of the people get the idea that they do not have to work because the other half is going to take care of them, and when the other half gets the idea that it does no good to work, because somebody else is going to get what they work for, that my dear friend, is the beginning of the end of any nation.

CHAPTER 50

IDENTITY THEFT

Thanks to the many kind folks in the banking industry, who had shown interest in me and my work ethics, I was well trained in different departments of the industry. All of that was well documented on my resume since it seemed I needed to put to use more often then wanted to, due to the many mergers in banking industry, specially the major ones like the good old Security Pacific, First Interstate and Great Western banks, to name a few. For some unexplained reason, smaller banking institution's compensations were more generous and the last bank where I landed a position the best way I knew how to (networking, there I go again with the good folks) certainly met the above category. I was informed that my perspective boss to be was a homosexual, and quite honestly I was not sure what I was supposed to do with that information. Frankly, I was even a little annoyed at the involuntary conversation about someone's sexuality before even meeting him. The interview was quite different from all the others in a good way. He was very professional yet completely non formal and immediately put me at ease. Within a short and sweet conversation, a detailed position offer with company benefits lay in front of me (to my surprise) pending the follow up formality of references, run of my credit report from all three agencies and something new to me, a background security check. The positives certainly outweighed any reason I might have had in mind not to take this offer and following my instincts felt right, so I did something I had never done before, telling him I would gladly accept the position. Notification of the results from the above verification would get to me via mail in a few days. Did not even give it a second thought to the formality of the background check or running of my credit report, since I had nothing to worry about, at least what I thought. Before the arrival of the results, I received a phone call from the ex co-worker, who had kindly referred me to the position, informing me, through the CEO of the bank, that there was a discrepancy on the background check with my social security number. Before jumping to any conclusion, my first thought was on how the company CEO had decided to get involved in the matter in the first place. I was so pleased with his character before even meeting him. Anna simply explained that the outcome of the background check had produced two names registered under the Social Security number I had provided, mine and another Latin woman's. To put my mind at ease, with a smile in her voice Anna told me about the conversation between her and Mr. Feldman (the CEO), who wanted to know if there was the probability of the other name through a different marriage. Anna explained to Mr. Feldman that the thought was very unlikely, because Armenians (Anna is also an Armenian from Iran) typically stuck to one marriage. Bottom line was that I, through my social security number was a victim of an identity theft going back to the eighties… It was hard to believe, because I only heard about identity theft happening to others. Naturally I was real upset. This could jeopardize my employment opportunity. The bank wanted me to file a police report and a written explanation of my identity with proof of different identification, such as original document of my U.S. Citizenship and my Driver's License, which I provided immediately. I was also strongly advised to block access to all three credit report agencies. Thank God the social security number was only used for employment purposes and not for credit card fraud. Not that employment fraud was not a big deal! Unsuccessfully, I placed numerous phone calls to the Employment Development Department for any helpful information on the fake individual, the criminal. I also discovered that millions of illegal workers were using stolen social security numbers and again the system was failing its citizens! Thankfully all of this was put behind (kind of) after many hours spent on my part without an arrest of the perpetrator. I began my employment, which meant health insurance coverage for me and my family. I was jubilant! Nervousness with a new job on a first day was almost nonexistent at this stage in my life. Full credit will be rewarded to experience. I was not marketing myself for career advancement, since I had the most rewarding and important role in life, wife and a mother. My philosophy on career versus family is controversial, either one or the other. Over many years I have seen career women's families crumble. The price is paid by children. This topic can be argued until I turn blue! Oh I hear mouthful from the liberal women and I am staying my ground! Call me old fashion, but this is my stand. However, having said that, I did take my position with the bank very seriously. The agreement was made for what I thought was a fair offer, especially the health insurance benefits; since my husband was self employed, I always provided the family health benefits through my employer. I had watched over the years those benefits shrink in size; though I still firmly believed it was impossible to live without, just as some women find impossible to live without certain brands of clothing or articles. As far as I was concerned, things would be no different at this job. Disciplined and professional is how I would conduct myself just as I had learned was best way to be at a workplace.

Some individuals give us the nonchalant gift of kindness and make a lifelong impact very deep inside, that is indescribable. I had the privilege to work for this person and called him "boss". Yes, this is the homosexual (gay) gentleman my interview was conducted with. Previously I had never given it a second thought about one's sexuality nor did I honestly care. As much as I believed in separation of work and personal relations it became impossible during my mom's illness and the support I received from him, gave me the courage to open up a dialogue about homosexuality and ask some simple questions. What I discovered over time, it is a very complicated subject to discuss. I, for myself have come to completely accept the fact, yet still have a hard time understanding the biological side of the issue. I much rather keep sexual life where it belongs, behind closed bedroom doors for both heterosexuals and homosexuals! He made it very clear to me, his interest in the same sex was from the very beginning of his youth and it was very hard for him to comprehend as well.

Finally what I wanted to clarify is in my perspective, it is much harder for most people to easily accept or understand homosexuality. Since the beginning of humanity, mankind has only known one partnership, between a man and a woman! And the unity of such has produced humanity, literally. So we need to be very cautious about this delicate issue, especially around children. We do not want to rob them of the very short and innocent childhood they have.

Like most folks in this country, I have a job. I work, they pay me. I pay my taxes and the government distributes my taxes as it sees fit. In order to get that paycheck, in my case, I am required to pass a random urine test(with which I have no problem). What I do have a problem with is the distribution of my taxes to people who don't have to pass a urine test. So, here is my question: Shouldn't one have to pass a urine test to get a welfare check? Because I have to pass one to earn it for them? Please understand, I have no problem with helping people get back on their feet. I do, on the other hand, have a problem with helping someone sit on their BUTT doing drugs while I work. Can you imagine how much money each state would save if people had to pass a urine test to get a public assistance check? I guess we could call the program
"URINE OR YOU'RE OUT"!

It takes twenty years to become an overnight success.

EDDIE CANTOR

CHAPTER 51

READING STIMULATES THE BRAIN

Entrepreneurial success is a gift with the very determined few. The fact is that the possibility of that success has been made possible under the protection of the U.S. Constitution formed by the founding fathers for countless immigrants coming to the land of the free in order to pursue that happiness/success, more than anywhere in the entire universe. No one can argue that. It is simply a fact. In our lifetime we come across those individuals mainly through media, such as the paper, the television, the radio and my favorite of all, books. Unfortunately and sadly for the upcoming generation(s) the radical shift in the media to glorify the brainless through reality shows and others alike has become common, more and more today. To study real gifted people had become a fascination for me for learning purposes and it took me very long time to realize that I did not have to look far at all for a serious encouragement/mentor. In fact, he lived with me under the same roof and I was married to him. This discovery was one of the biggest puzzles that had come together and I was going to take full advantage to study the success of this man's secret in business. College education is the first on the dismissal list, because he certainly is not, yet he is running a small successful retail store in an upper middle class suburban area in Ventura County and his customers simply adore him and his craftsmanship. This information was not passed on to me through him, but every opportunity time allowed, I got involved in his business and watched and analyzed and learned. What has fascinated me the most about his character is his strong belief in himself and his work ethics. It is fair to say that living with my husband for almost three decades is a reasonably long time to truly understand him on a deeper level. I don't ever recall him calling in sick, regardless of when he worked for someone else or himself. Ever since self employed, he jokes about trying to call in sick and says the line just rings and rings and no one picks up on the other end. Sure he has gotten sick with the common cold or the flu, and other minor stuff in between, yet has gotten himself up very optimistic (certainly a morning person, not so optimistic in the evenings though) and when asked about his well being his answer is almost always the same with a broad smile curving his thick and perfect lips, making him even more handsome, "great". It almost is like this man's outlook, specifically when it comes to his business, is programmed like a happy robot that lacks anything other. The conclusion I have come to believe his secret, is putting himself out with people as genuine, never trying anything but with English language echoing very clearly for everyone as his second language very unapologetically. In return, his customers have embraced his honesty and as a token of appreciation have spread the good word about this young, old fashioned jeweler with highest moral values. Some even call him a magician, others keep telling me what a good man he is and I am grateful and take those words as the biggest compliments and other times I choke up with the thank you's. What really makes him special in my eyes is his giving to his customers through minor repairs of jewelry and watches. I try to be a smart advisor and tell him to stop fixing and repairing things right then and there so we can charge something, anything!

I remind him that (like he needs reminding) we are in business for profit and we have to make a living. His looks are priceless and all I can do is laugh, which makes him madder.

Over the years we have come to know hundreds if not thousands of families in this peaceful town, and the unfamiliar ones who walk in through the door almost always comment that so and so sent them to us, which never gets old. On the contrary, it is a validation of our hard honest work. On one of these occasions a very attractive lady walked into our store and after spending a few minutes glancing at the showcases (another important tip he has taught me to never approach the customers immediately, but give them few minutes to breath, which truly works) inquired about a sterling silver ring to only find out that would not fit on her fingers (she tried on more than one). Knowing a thing or two about sizing sterling silver rings, I informed her that this particular ring was not sizable, and to validate my statement I walked to the master jeweler with the ring in my hand. While I was explaining the request, the lady with a mischievous voice yelled out since he was in the back room " I am confident you can do it, that's the word out there that you repair the impossible, you are the magician". Her charm worked with a condition. She was explained that there would be a good chance of all the stones that were set on the ring could burn. With her agreement I jotted her name and phone number on a repair envelope and promised to call her within a day or two with the outcome of the repair. She repeated her beliefs in my husband's skills and left. When I phoned her with the good news about the readiness of the ring, her answering machine identified her as an author of some book that I could not quite comprehend the title. Nevertheless I was very excited to know that this woman was an author. I informed my husband about the discovery and could not wait for her visit so we could chat about her book. Within few hours of the phone call, Cynthia half appeared at the entrance and Albert from the back room of the store recognizing her through the camera yelled out "where is my signed copy". She turned right back and said that she had a copy in the car and appeared back within moments with a book in her hand titled "Unstoppable Women" by Cynthia Kersy. After a long chat with this amazing woman I could not wait to know more about her through the book with a title that spoke volumes.

Sit down dinners have always been and always will be an important part of our family. It is a traditional Armenian value that has been passed down from the beginning and thankfully for most of Armenian homes very much alive. Every night within an hour of us getting home between my husband and me, we sit down to a homemade aromatic, mainly Mediterranean feast. I find cooking relaxing enjoyment sipping on a glass of red wine (only one). This particular evening, Cynthia's book in mind; I could not wait to finish dinner. Actually for once I decided not to care about the dirty dishes, and opening the book while standing by the counter of our kitchen and a while later finding myself very tired from standing in high heel shoes and sitting my butt on the stool chair near the counter, I startled myself from the loud noise of my shoes falling on the tile floor. The microwave clock read 1:00 a.m. and there were few more pages left to finish this fascinating woman's true story.

You cannot legislate the poor into prosperity, by legislating the wealth out of prosperity.
What one person receives without working for, another person must work for without receiving.
The government cannot give to anybody anything that the government does not first take from somebody else.
You cannot multiply wealth by dividing it.

CHAPTER 52

PRIVATE SECTOR VERSES GOVERNMENT

Finishing this incredible book (Unstoppable Women) was the beginning of my courage to open a dialogue with everyday ordinary folks about my idea of a book, my strong point of views about the land of the free. It would be the perspective of a young immigrant teenager coming to United States at the age of fifteen and very confused about her identity. It was expected by our elders for me and all the young generation kids that had immigrated into this county to be an Armenian and nothing else, and the reason for it was crystal clear. Armenians were persecuted over many centuries by bordering Muslim countries with devastating results, so survival with an identity had become an Armenian mission. After all, the biggest blow to our race was the genocide by the Turkish government, for literally slaughtering over one and a half million Armenians, that almost cost us our existence. And the Turks are still shamelessly denying it. If I could, I would hire a Jewish Private Relations (a morning radio personality on KFI, AM station, walk of fame Bill Handel comes to mind) for this almost one hundred year old unresolved tragedy! I have been listening to Handel for at least a dozen years and he has made my morning drives, even during heavy traffic, pleasurable (sometimes laughing out loud). His office is in the heart of an Armenian community and he claims to almost have gotten into a fist fight over the Armenian genocide issue with a Turk (which I have no reason not to believe). The Jews have accomplished, well deserved results, with the holocaust. Actually, when Hitler was on his monstrous mission, on one of his addresses he had said, and I quote "Who remembers the extermination of the Armenians"? The evidence on the Armenian genocide is overwhelming, yet for strong political reasons, we cannot bring this issue to justice, once and for all!

Throughout the world, Armenians have accomplished the unthinkable with them carrying the Holy Cross of Christian/Apostolic, strong traditional values. (Armenians are the first race to accept Christianity). There are astronomical differences between Christian traditional Armenians from the west portion of what used to be Armenian land, which is under Turkish control currently, and the eastern Armenians from the previous Soviet Union, who have immigrated to the United Stated in the last two decades. The Communist/Atheists through brutality and fear were successful in short few decades to wipe out all of Christianity. These people who ran Armenia under strict Soviet guidelines and taught us in schools that there is no God, that Lenin (one of the leaders of communism) was, and that United States of America was the evil capitalistic empire. These Godless (Ann Coulter line, perfectly suitable for the subject, literally) people were the ones discriminating against their own people every opportunity they got, simply because of our parents' Christian/traditional beliefs and the fact that they had migrated from Europe or the Middle East to live on their own land. Guess what, all those who constantly mocked us and made fun of us for leaving communist Armenia tried to pour into the United States. And not just from Armenia, but all other nationalities from all fifteen republics of the previous Soviet Union. To clarify it little further, most either applied for a tourist visa and never left the county or applied for a fake asylum or somehow came to Mexico and crossed the border illegally. Not much was left to be taken from the old communism and now it was going to be tried in the good old United States. Kennedy's greatest speech had an opposite meaning "it is not what you can do for the country, but what the country can do for you". And the sadness of it all, United States was not even their country. These new want to be Americans were very choosy and picky. They wanted nothing to do with a loyalty to this great Nation, but what was in it for them! Wow, communism created greedy monsters! These are sad facts. Thousands of them have split up their families, husbands and wives, here illegally, alone, not seen their children or their spouses in years. Above all, they have completely lost themselves in all human values and morals, robbing their children and or spouses of their presence. The meaning of family has disappeared into the thin air, like colorful balloons, that cannot hold their own!

In addition to the millions of dependants in the land of the free, millions more were added after the collapse of the Soviets. Many newcomers have managed to receive some form of financial assistance, (thanks to our liberal politicians) whether it is welfare for children, section 8, that covers something like 70% of monthly rent, and most over 65 years of age receive Social Security income with a government paid caretaker and the list goes on and on and on (like the energizer battery commercial). I can only imagine the amount of heat I am going to get for this chapter (story of my life in the political arena). There will be a lot of applause though! Doing the right thing is the best medicine for the heart and the mind. In my simple and humble opinion the data on this chapter is a tiny fraction of the corruption that goes on in most states, especially in once famous state of California. It is time to stop the madness. If our politicians continue to allow the "poor people" to financially rape the American taxpayer, we don't need to fear natural disaster but a financial one. I wanted to find my identity under the U.S. constitution and clarify it to tens of millions of immigrants the purpose of all of us migrating to this land discovered by the great minds of the founding fathers.

First of all, this book would (hopefully) give me the opportunity to be part of the free capitalistic world where I will contribute twenty percent of proceeds from all sales to our military, which protect the very freedom that is so fragile right now. The power of individual giving is fascinating beyond words. Instead of the government deciding where one's earnings go, it's the sole discretion of the individual. Wow! If that is not wonder of freedom I don't know what is. Not too long ago, my immigrant parents were at the end of the receiving line and that was very degrading and depressing for me. The decision about donating to the military was made in my head long before I even knew I was capable of writing a book.

This project did not seem unreachable any longer. The amount of moral support from the American people about my story was nothing short of a miracle. In the recent handful of years I was on full time basis working at my husband's retail store. This is where I had the privilege to converse with the everyday folks, whom, out of frustration openly discussed politics, which gave me the opportunity and the courage to do the same. One particular individual befriended me by a sheer coincidence, to say the least. This gorgeous blond with beautiful long hair, tall and slender (did I mention gorgeous) woman was a regular customer and every time she walked into our retail shop, I was very intimidated by her presence! As time went by so did my confidence level's measurement in the positive direction. I became much more comfortable in my own skin, to a point where we became friends and our love for nature and the outdoors gave me the opportunity to hike with Jennifer couple of times a week. During our hikes we shared life experiences and she thought mine needed to be on paper, without any knowledge of my book idea. At the time Jennifer was going through personal tough times and this highly educated and sophisticated woman, who looked like she was cut out of a magazine naturally, without make up, was telling me how much our conversations had helped her in a positive direction, and kept thanking me for coming into her life! I could not believe it. Her encouragement had sealed my book deal in my head.

My humble story and the major changes in this country merged together in harmony. Almost every new chapter began with doubts and overcoming it, was challenging, though somehow my strong belief for freedom carried me through and made it possible to continue. I pleasantly surprised myself at the end of some chapters and others just were not so.

I should like to see any power of the world destroy this race, this small tribe of unimportant people, whose wars have all been fought and lost, whose structures have crumbled, literature is unread, music is unheard, and prayers are no more answered. Go ahead, destroy Armenia. See if you can do it. Send them into the desert without bread or water. Burn their homes and churches. Then see if they will not laugh, sing and pray again. For when two of them meet anywhere in the world, see if they will not create a New Armenia.

WILLIAM SAROYAN

CHAPTER 53

PROUD TO CALL MYSELF AMERICAN ARMENIAN

The truth is always painful; thus, acceptance and realization of the truth is critical for a peaceful and meaningful life. Making excuses for people or situations that are inexcusable irritates me immensely, like the ones mentioned in the above chapters. Thank God, for all the bad ones out there who disgrace humanity, there are millions of honorable, decent and successful people all over the United States and the world, who make me so proud to call myself an American Armenian. Just a few come to mind who have been part of my inspiration to write this book, whose families through immigration, just like mine, have come to America to pursue the happiness promised in the United States Constitution. The talented author / dramatist / academy award winner for best story "The Human Comedy" William Saroyan, whose brilliant work has been honored by the United States and USSR's postal service by putting his photo on a stamp, who's refusal of the Pulitzer prize for drama in 1940, has impressed and taught me immensely. George Deukmejian, the "Duke" who successfully governed the state of California from 1983 through 1991. The very private and humble billionaire, Kirk Kerkorian, nickname "Godfather of Las Vegas", whose entrepreneurial skills simply amaze me. There is an endless list of the last names ending with "ian or yan", whose successes have been made possible in the free world. The point I am hoping the reader to comprehend is the endless possibilities of an individual success is made possible through our constitution, the founding fathers so brilliantly put together over about two centuries ago and during that time, under that simple yet important document more successes have been produced by individuals than anywhere in the entire world over thousands of years. Oh can't forget this one! That my fellow reader, IS the American exceptionalism! (please read this sentence several times). So whether Armenian, Italian, Jewish, Irish, African American, Latino or any other nationality, acceptance with an embrace of this wonderful country and its people is the beginning of any success in this land of the free. Do you know that over one hundred years American middle class family has dominated the world and American currency (the US Dollar) rocked the world! You know why? Immigrants proudly became Americans. In fact when World War II broke and first generation immigrants went to fight for this country, proudly carried one flag, the American flag. The meaning of immigration surely has changed since when I was brought to this country with many hopes and dreams.

I carefully chose the above famous quote from the Saroyan library, so everyone can understand that they do not have to give up their individuality, nor being American means or suggests in any way to deny your race. It simply means that you have to honor those who fought and continue to fight the battle of freedom to capture the United States of America by being American first.

Those who make the worst use of their time are the first to complain of its shortness.

JEAN DE LA BRUYERE, 17TH CENTURY FRENCH ESSAYIST

CHAPTER 54

FORTIES HAD DONE WONDERS FOR ME

Life has become so beautifully meaningful that the thought is overwhelming at times. All the positive people with genuine smiles, the endless meaningful quotations I read, many-many great books, and of course Dr. Laura have shaped me into a strong and positive individual, who has learned to live life to its fullest. Those darn endorphins work their magic every morning after an hour and a half of power walk. I have finally come to terms and embraced my body. Couple of weeks ago warm and humid days in late October were making my morning walks quite uncomfortable yet cutting it short was out of the question. So in a midst of a moment I looked up to the sky and wished for a heavy downpour of a rain. What do you know, a few days later (I looked up again into the sky and thanked God for his generosity) my wish was granted and there was a downpour of a rain outside making its presence by dancing down on my windows. Just as I was getting ready for my walk my husband ask me with a surprised look on his face "you are not walking today, are you?" My answer to him "I prayed for this rain". You can call it a coincidence and I will call it an answer to my small request/prayer. Nonetheless, I thought "what a shame I am the only one enjoying this magnificent walk", umbrella in one hand, a big bottle of water in the other. Today I decide not to listen to music through my I-pod my son gave me last Christmas. I want to enjoy the natural sounds of the rain. I am not an electronics person, but the music I have downloaded on this tiny box called the shuffle, with the help of my children. I do thank the genius behind this tiny box almost every morning (sometimes I forget) as I push the little "on" button and the miracle of several hundred songs is literally ready for my enjoyment at my fingertips. There are pretty much all kinds of songs/music in the shuffle yet the classical symphony of Beethoven, Shopen, or Chikovski to name a few turn my power walks into runs. I never knew running was something my legs were capable of. At the end of the five (5) mile walk/run, a pleasant smile broadens my energized face with the strong traces clearly visible throughout the rest of the day. I do thank my mother for her insistence on my musical education and my very patient piano teacher, who believed in me when I did not for the love of the classical music!

Don't say you don't have enough time. You have exactly the same number of hours per day that were given to Helen Keller, Pasteur, Michelangelo, Mother Teresa, Leonardo de Vinci, Thomas Jefferson, and Albert Einstein.

H. JACKSON BROWN

CHAPTER 55

FREEDOM DEFINED

Traditional values have their roots deep within me like an old oak tree standing solid in the soil. The proof is clearly in our home, especially in the kitchen, where my evenings begin preparing homemade, mostly Mediterranean meals with the staples of my kitchen of cold pressed olive oil, garlic, onions and variety of fresh herbs and vegetables. A glass of red wine, olives and assorted chesses complete our table each evening. With my husband's involvement, and little bit of love, we sit down to a delectable dinner in about an hour. What really makes every moment worthwhile is when my teenage daughter walks home through the front door, making her presence very loud and clear and comments something about the good aromas of the food and asks of me to share the recipe of just about everything I make! Her comment tops off any compliment or recognition I can ask or imagine.

Eight o'clock weeknights Mr. Bill O'Reilly gets my undivided attention for an hour and when available my daughter joins me on the couch for an hour of informative and bold dialogue. She bombards me with many questions and I always have to remind her to hold them until the annoying commercial breaks come along. She does not stop there and wants to tell me about her daily social life that pertains to the reporting from the "Factor". Her emotions take the best of her when she starts on one specific professor's teachings of sociology. Ironically this middle age fellow is Armenian from the previous Soviet Union just like me, and has radical socialistic views and does not think very highly of capitalistic system. He miserably fails by attempting to make all his students believe that he will never let them see his political views. Handful of students in his class from about forty will challenge him on his opinionated statements, including my daughter. He passively dismisses their legitimate questions by playing the good old "it is possible" scenario and moves on to proof other disturbing untrue issues. One of his unprofessional statements just the other day was about how the Fox News reporters are all liars and naturally my daughter wants to prove him wrong yet does not have what it takes to stand up to a lying uninformed professor. My strong advice to her or anybody who cares about the political truth is find out for yourself. Thank goodness for today's technology, do your own research. And my take on the subject is, for the love of this country, we owe it to the founders of the free world, or you can follow the footsteps of the naïve students from progressive professors that fill many universities today. Another option, yet an expensive and dangerous one, travel to Iran or North Korea. Or to save a bundle of money, why not, lot closer to our not so friendly communist Cuban neighbor and see it for yourself how much value or freedom one's life has if you do not follow the government's rules. Our skies are not so friendly with Cuban skies (and with a good reason) but it can be done through Mexico. To travel just about anywhere in the world is part of our, taken for granted freedom. Results, in my opinion, you will become an instant patriotic American, maybe even kiss the ground when your foot touches it. And for some crazy reason, you do not agree with my assessment, under the same freedom you can definitely move from this country anywhere in the globe, unlike those, who would give their only shirt to come to the United States of America.

A man who wants something will find a way; a man who doesn't will find an excuse.

STEPHEN DOLLEY, JR

CHAPTER 56

MATURITY

The above simple yet powerful quotation is taped on my computer desktop and after my quiet Morning Prayer and gratitude to God, I read these words of wisdom and my day begins. Reflection of that historic day back in January of 1981, immigrating to United States has become stronger over time. The precious goals and dreams each and every member of my family so delicately carried in our hearts and minds, for most of us was aborted at its infancy, in my opinion.

My time on the computer is minimal due to hectic schedule between work and family, and I like it just the way it is; however, I receive e-mails from good friends and spend few minutes reading some of them. Most are informative, inspirational, spiritual or funny, so I forward them to specific friends, who I know will appreciate a short good read. This is one of those, where after reading it several times I decided lot more people must read and comprehend the silent (not so silent, sometimes) revolution that is taking place in the our country!

"I'M 63 AND I'M TIRED"
By Robert A. Hall

I'm 63. Except for one semester in college when jobs were scarce and a six-month period when I was between jobs, but job-hunting every day, I've worked, hard, since I was 18. Despite some health challenges, I still put in 50-hour weeks, and haven't called in sick in seven or eight years. I make a good salary, but I didn't inherit my job or my income, and I worked to get where I am. Given the economy, there's no retirement in sight, and I'm tired. Very tired.

I'm tired of being told that I have to "spread the wealth" to people who don't have my work ethic. I'm tired of being told the government will take the money I earned, by force if necessary, and give it to people too lazy to earn it.

173

I'm tired of being told that Islam is a "Religion of Peace," when every day I can read dozens of stories of Muslim men killing their sisters, wives and daughters for their family "honor"; of Muslims rioting over some slight offense; of Muslims murdering Christian and Jews because they aren't "believers"; of Muslims burning schools for girls; of Muslims stoning teenage rape victims to death for "adultery"; of Muslims mutilating the genitals of little girls; all in the name of Allah, because the Qur'an and Shari'a law tells them to.

I'm tired of being told that out of "tolerance for other cultures" we must let Saudi Arabia use our oil money to fund mosques and madrasa Islamic schools to preach hate in America and Canada , while no American nor Canadian group is allowed to fund a church, synagogue or religious school in Saudi Arabia to teach love and tolerance.

I'm tired of being told I must lower my living standard to fight global warming, which no one is allowed to debate.

I'm tired of being told that drug addicts have a disease, and I must help support and treat them, and pay for the damage they do. Did a giant germ rush out of a dark alley, grab them, and stuff white powder up their noses while they tried to fight it off?

I'm tired of hearing wealthy athletes, entertainers and politicians of both parties talking about innocent mistakes, stupid mistakes or youthful mistakes, when we all know they think their only mistake was getting caught. I'm tired of people with a sense of entitlement, rich or poor.

I'm real tired of people who don't take responsibility for their lives and actions. I'm tired of hearing them blame the government, or discrimination or big-whatever for their problems.

Yes, I'm damn tired. But I'm also glad to be 63. Because, mostly, I'm not going to have to see the world these people are making. I'm just sorry for my granddaughter.

Robert A. Hall is a Marine Vietnam veteran who served five terms in the Massachusetts State Senate.

"Never complain about growing old, far too many people have been denied that privilege".

CHAPTER 57

IS AMERICAN FREEDOM AT STAKE?

Freedom is never more than one generation away from extinction. We didn't pass it to our children in the bloodstream. It must be fought for, protected, and handed on for them to do the same, or one day we will spend our sunset years telling our children and our children's children what it was once like in the United States where men were free.

Ronald Reagan, 40th President

One of the greatest quotes written by one of the greatest president, sends chills down my spine every time I read it. If patriotic Americans don't stand up against political correctness in this country, I am afraid that precious freedom that is the greatest gift from the genius founding fathers to the American people will become the thing of the past and the entire world will suffer greatly.

Lisa U. Vartanian

Author of *"Price and Power of Freedom"*

My great grandfather watched as his friends died in the Civil War, my grandfather watched as his friends died in WW II, and my father watched as my friends died in Vietnam.

None of them died for the Mexican Flag.

Everyone died for the U.S. flag.

In Texas, a student raised a Mexican flag on a school flag pole; another student took it down. Guess who was expelled...the kid who took it down.

Kids in high school in California were sent home this year on Cinco de Mayo because they wore T-shirts with the American flag printed on them.

Enough is enough.

These wise words needs to be read by every American; and every American needs to stand up for America

We've bent over to appease the America-haters long enough.

I'm taking a stand.

I'm standing up because the hundreds of thousands who died fighting in wars for this country, and for the U.S. flag can't stand up.

And shame on anyone who tries to make this a racist message.

Let me make this perfectly clear!

THIS IS MY COUNTRY!

And, because I make This statement

DOES NOT

Mean I'm against immigration!!!

YOU ARE WELCOME HERE, IN MY COUNTRY!

Welcome! To come through legally:

1. Get a sponsor!

2. Get a place to lay your head!

3.Get a job!

4. Live By OUR Rules!

5. Pay YOUR Taxes!

and

6. Learn the LANGUAGE like immigrants have in the past!!!

AND

7. Please don't demand that we hand over our lifetime savings of Social Security Funds to you.

When will AMERICANS STOP giving away THEIR RIGHTS???

We've gone so far the other way... bent over backwards not to offend anyone.

But it seems no one cares about the

AMERICAN CITIZEN

That's being offended!

WAKE UP America !!!

ANANIMUS WAR VETERAN

Then you will know the truth, and the truth will set you free.
John 8:32

I want to thank my husband from the bottom of my heart for his hard working ethics. My kind, conservative children for never giving me much trouble. My daughter-in-law, who has become a part of our family and made me look beautiful on the cover of this book by her talented make-up work.

Special thanks to Mark and Beverly Schlechters. Without their assistance, this book would not have been possible! Many thanks to Jennifer Slocum for her belief in me, when I did not believe in myself. And above all, I want to thank every individual, who has encouraged me to finish my story and promised to support my final product. Your encouragements were the force behind this book.

Made in the USA
Middletown, DE
03 March 2023

25991391R00106